Ingrid Horrocks did her PhD at Princeton and teaches creative writing at Massey University, Wellington, where she lives with her partner and two daughters. Her previous books include *Travelling with Augusta, Women Wanderers and the Writing of Mobility* and two collections of poetry. With Cherie Lacey, she is the co-editor of *Extraordinary Everywhere*. She is a member of the NonfictioNOW International Board and a contributing NZ-Aotearoa editor to the *Sydney Review of Books*.

Also by Ingrid Horrocks

Natsukashii (Pemmican Press, 1998)

Travelling with Augusta: Preston–Gorizia–Venice–Masterton, 1835 & 1999 (VUP, 2003)

Mapping the Distance (VUP, 2010)

Women Wanderers and the Writing of Mobility, 1784–1814 (Cambridge University Press, 2017)

As editor

Letters Written during a Short Residence in Sweden, Norway, and Denmark, by Mary Wollstonecraft (Broadview Press, 2013)

Charlotte Smith: Major Poetic Works
(with Claire Knowles, Broadview Press, 2017)

Extraordinary Anywhere: Essays on Place from Aotearoa New Zealand (with Cherie Lacey, VUP, 2017)

Where We Swim

Explorations of nature, travel and family

INGRID HORROCKS

First published 2021 by Victoria University of Wellington Press
This edition published 2021 by University of Queensland Press
PO Box 6042, St Lucia, Queensland 4067 Australia

uqp.com.au
reception@uqp.com.au

Cover design by Christabella Designs
Author photograph by Ebony Lamb
Typeset in Heldane Text 11.5/16pt
Printed in Australia by McPherson's Printing Group

A catalogue record for this book is available from the National Library of Australia.

ISBN 978 0 7022 6340 8 (pbk)
ISBN 978 0 7022 6534 1 (epdf)
ISBN 978 0 7022 6535 8 (epub)
ISBN 978 0 7022 6536 5 (kindle)

University of Queensland Press uses papers that are natural, renewable and recyclable products made from wood grown in well-managed forests and other controlled sources. The logging and manufacturing processes conform to the environmental regulations of the country of origin.

MIX
Paper from
responsible sources
FSC   FSC® C001695
www.fsc.org

For my fluid family
in all its breadth and strangeness.

Contents

Immersing

Gone Swimming

I was drawn to the wide open mouth of the river, the place where it took in the sea. It was a beautiful day, with a pale blue sky, the sea hardly moving, the water gleaming smooth in the sun. The night before, the woman at the Mōkau petrol station had recommended I swim on the estuary's incoming morning tide for cleaner, clearer water.

As I stepped in, I felt the river's tug. At first I walked upstream with the tide, waist-deep and two metres from shore. Then I lay on my back, toes poking out, hands fluttering like vestigial wings, and let myself drift, water lapping around my ears. For a while I closed my eyes, letting the tide carry me, feeling the press of the water's echoey breath. As the minutes stretched, the water seemed to enter my body, my limbs becoming liquid.

Then at the bend, the current pulled me away from the edge. I flipped and reached for the bottom but it had dropped away and the water moved fast and straight, tugging at my legs as I tried to kick myself back. My arms hardly made headway against the pull, my panicked strokes almost useless against it.

Only just before the rush right out to the centre of the river did I manage to push my feet down and hit a sandbar. First just my toes touched, trying to hook in, till the sandy riverbed rose up. Then I was standing, half my body above water again, able to resist its

1

swift movements. Breathing hard, I looked ahead to the expanse of river where the wide, fast-flowing waters were headed. I waded carefully along the bar back to shore.

A woman in gumboots was fishing in the shallows, her line stretching across my route. I got out of the water and stood there dripping, letting the sun warm my skin.

She was catching kahawai mainly, she said, but sometimes she got trevally or snapper.

'Do you swim?' I asked.

'Well . . .' She paused. 'I prefer swimming pools. Besides, I know what's in here.'

Together we stood and looked across the rapidly running water, undergoing its twice-daily cleansing which could never be enough.

It was early autumn 2017, and I was swimming my way from Wellington to Auckland. I'd taken a long weekend, fitted between teaching classes, to drive north and swim alone in as many places as I could along the way.

Not that I can really swim. That's why the river almost got me. On swimming sports days at high school, I was that kid at the back of the race who was more drowning than swimming. I'm not confident I'd meet the common definition of being able to swim, which is swimming 200 metres of freestyle in a pool. Even Lake Dudding in the Rangitīkei was heavy-going, and it's a very small lake. I'd just walked around its perimeter and done my own version of awkward breaststroke across a corner so I could feel what it was like to swim with a destination. As a swimmer, I have few aspirations to mastery. But I've always loved being in water, baths included. In setting out, I wanted to know what that was about. I'd wanted to remember why it was we swam in the first place. And to remember the pleasure of immersing in an element other than air.

The year 2017 was also when everyone seemed to start using the word 'swimmable'. Which of our rivers and lakes were swimmable? How many of our beaches? Which weren't? Where would the water make us and our children (and parents) sick? My impulse to swim in as many places as I could had been prompted, in part, by playing with a new website called 'Can I Swim Here?' Before I set off, I'd printed out water-quality maps, on which rivers that were rated 'Excellent' or 'Good' appeared in blue and green, merging into the paper landscapes. They were the colours of water. They were the fantasy tones of childhood and tourism campaigns. But in many areas, especially the rural ones, the yellow, orange and red of 'Fair' or 'Poor' water quality threaded out from the maps' mountain centres like cancer cells, darkening as the waters dropped from the hills and began their journeys through human and farm animal country to the sea.

I hadn't looked at the maps closely before planning my route. I planned mainly based on scenic photographs. I only began to study the maps along the way, and by the time I swam at Mōkau, on the upper Taranaki Bight, I knew the river's Waikato catchment was home to 440,000 sheep, 70,000 beef cattle and 20,000 dairy cattle. The whole length of the river threaded its way across the maps in blood red, not even getting a blue mountain moment at its source.

My determination to swim anyway was partly a denial of those water-quality figures being the final word – a refusal to let that be how it would be, even here, in this country, the water already too polluted to bother. It was a refusal to accept and simply stay home on dry land. But perhaps it was also an attempt to understand those figures better, to translate backwards from abstractions such as counting rivers by length or by swimmability. An attempt to put my whole body into it. Perhaps it could serve as some form of animal engagement and involvement – of necessary immersion. What were those numbers really telling us? Or, more properly maybe, what were the waters saying? Perhaps I wanted to feel what it meant to swim so that I could imagine what was at stake in a place becoming unswimmable – for other creatures, too, who also need water to live.

A day after swimming at Mōkau I developed a urinary tract infection. The source of the infection could have been almost anywhere in the regions I'd swum, at least in the rivers and smaller lakes. It could also have been from too much time in clammy swimsuits. Even if not directly attributable, it *felt* like my body's physical response to the toxic water in some of the places I'd chosen to swim. My estuary swim wasn't what I'd planned or imagined, but it did help me understand. The numbers were serious. The water was too.

Before I set out, I'd swum with my family at Princess Bay, a hook of beach on the Taputeranga Marine Reserve on Wellington's south coast. By the time I arrived at Mōkau I'd paddled in small waves on the Kāpiti Coast, where my mother spent her summers in the 1950s. I'd swum in a fenced hotel pool. And I'd swum off the beach at Koitiata, just south of Whanganui, then in the Whanganui River itself.

I'd swum one early morning with a childhood friend in the Tokomaru River in the Manawatū. With my friends' kids as audience, we'd wobbled in on the grey river stones until we were waist-deep, hands held out and above the water, fingers splayed like stars. We were almost out before we were in, our skin humming with the chill of it, the feeling carrying some body memory of our years growing up together. The Tokomaru River also turned out to at times be 'Code Red', as in 'Avoid Swimming'. I'd somehow thought it must be all right, because it was up near the mountains, but there were E. coli warnings in place; that is, there were animal or human faeces in the water. According to the Ministry for the Environment, just 45 per cent of rivers by length in the Manawatū and Whanganui regions were generally 'swimmable', meaning 55 per cent were not. The shit levels in Lake Dudding were okay, but there was an intermittent risk of toxic algae from farm run-off. As I'd swum across it, I had to clear weed away from my face at each stroke.

I'd skinny-dipped below sandstone cliffs at Ototoka, becoming just a human figure stepping into the sea. Naked, I felt single and whole, not stripped into sections, some less publicly acceptable than others. As I went under in the ocean there, the undertow sucking at my body, I'd felt a childish Maurice Sendak-like rhyme running through me: *I am in the sea and the sea is in me.* It felt like a naïve version of the whakataukī 'Ko au te awa, ko te awa ko au'. 'I am the river, and the river is me.' News had been coming over the car radio every hour about the Treaty settlement which acknowledged that the Whanganui river had legal personhood – a recognition of the place of water in kaupapa Māori understandings. Māori have insisted on this all along: awa as living being. Before I swum, the day before, in the Whanganui, I'd stood waist-deep for a long time, wondering whether I should even be there. Swimming in an entity – in a person, even. In someone else's ancestor. The best I could make of it was to imagine it as a challenging, evolving relationship.

At some point in my solo swimming journey, I felt there was a problem with it. It sectioned off swimming and water, and ecology, from daily life. Swimming alone seemed not to get fully to the heart of things.

At the time, my twin daughters were seven, and it was a big deal to be driving away, to have time alone, stretched-out moments to drift. I'd been reading *Waterlog* by Roger Deakin, in which he recounts swimming through Britain's seas, rivers, lakes and fens in search of a 'frog's eye view', and it had made me dream of watery solitudes. I was excited to have an excuse to escape the intense combination of work and family for a time, and to turn my focus further outwards.

I can see now that in some ways my swimming journey was an extended version of the 5pm swims I took in my twins' first summer. I would head off the moment Tim got home from work, detaching myself from the sticky bodies of our daughters, and would drive over the hill and down to the beach at Hataitai. The swims were quick – out of the car, down the steps to the narrow strip of gravelly sand, and in and out of the water, as planes in the distance rose into the sky. There might have only been half a dozen 5pm swims, but the memory of being a single body carried elsewhere for a moment stayed with me. It was as though those swims helped to keep the whole enterprise afloat.

Still, even with the 5pm swims, much of the pleasure was in the return home. I would shower with the window open, Tim outside with our newly minted children on a blanket in the garden as they practised rolling over and toe sucking, harakeke sending out jubilant shoots that brought black sheeny flickers and clicks of tūī.

I wasn't about to underestimate the value of solitary escapes. But it felt important, too, to see that these were bracketed moments held deep within lives.

A solo swimming journey – and I'd at first imagined there being a series of these – ultimately felt too deliberate, too intentional, and too solitary. Too obvious even, at least to me, even while relatively peculiar to other people. In the end, it felt too close to the act of an explorer, or an old-school nature writer. I stopped paying attention to swimming and stopped writing about it.

Then, two years later, I realised I'd been swimming all along. Everywhere my family and I went, we swam. Swimming was right there at the breathing core of things – both the centre of family and a stroke away from it. All that casual tumbling into water felt like the place where swimming more often dwelt. Each swim in each place was all its own thing. I stopped being so literal, and the question of why we swim morphed into all sorts of other questions.

Without fully realising it, I seemed to have arrived in the middle of life, spending those two years swimming my way into the next phase, whatever that would be. I also became properly conscious of how the feel of the planet was shifting, and along with it, my always provisional sense of what it means to be alive in the world, as a grown-up daughter, a sister, a partner, a mother, and human animal living alongside other animals – sheep and cattle, whales and manatee, elks and ibises. The question didn't seem to be so much why we swim, as where and how we swim, and with whom. Also, where we fail to swim, water threatening to flood our lungs or the lungs of others, as well as where we rise and float.

We swam until we were made to stop. When Covid-19 arrived, when I was just about finished writing about swimming, the country entered lockdown but we were still able to walk streets and hills. The virus was hardly in this country yet, and we still have space. But we were locked on land, forbidden from entering the water, unable to take flight. For those five weeks we were grounded. As I write this, I am still waiting to see how things will be when we try swimming again – what we will make of our new mortality. It is seeming possible that the age of diasporic family connected by cheap ocean-crossing travels may be over. A two-century or two-decade bracket, depending on how you define it; either way, a blip in time. Where we swim for the foreseeable future looks likely to be from this island in our own green sea.

Back in the afternoon of my Mōkau swim in 2017, I drove on to Raglan. Driving through patches of bush among cleared hills, I remembered both the stark loveliness of the hills on the Wairarapa sheep farm where I grew up, and how it takes a hundred years for the roots of big trees to rot. I thought about the ghost roots of the nineteenth-century bush clearances holding the skeletons of these hills in place. There had been heavy rains in the weeks before I drove through, and three weeks afterwards further downpours from a tropical cyclone would cause floods and massive slips, closing the road. I was lucky, incommensurably lucky in so many ways.

I arrived in Raglan as sun glazed the estuary golden. I pitched my tent in the campground on the tip of the peninsula. After dinner in town, I went out in the dark thinking I'd have a final swim, a night swim, but as soon as I put my feet into the estuary I felt mud. It sucked around my toes in a way that wasn't quite liquid. I'd have had more success at the surf beach around the corner. Another 20 metres on it was still ankle-deep, while way ahead sandbars rose above the surface. I walked on, not swimming this time, but walking the water's terrain. The only sound was the splash of my feet rising and falling.

It was a moonless night but the way the water had drained away reminded me of the force of the moon's gravitational pull. Above me there were more stars every minute it seemed, although perhaps it was just my eyes adjusting. And then I saw, or at least thought I saw, the stars reflected on the water. Could light be thrown down from the sky like that? In the sky the stars blurred into the arching haze of the Milky Way, but in the water just the brightest of them gleamed. I felt then the smallness of this planet, with its seas and tributaries, its veins of rivers and lakes. And the brevity of the time we have. I could be standing on the back of a whale swimming in the sky.

Days Bay

Marvellous here. Come n swim.

Wellington Anniversary weekend, we drove the half hour from our house around the harbour to Days Bay, then up the road to my parents' place on the edge of the hill, where in the quiet of stream and bush sounds it felt as though we were far from the city. Then it was a cup of tea (always), everyone talking at once, my parents with something to show Tim and me, the kids heading off to get the soft toys that lived there with their grandparents. The weather seemed perfect.

At a gathering a while ago, family friends had told me that my parents seemed decades younger than the rest of them. As we drove out, I was aware of the intensity with which I wanted this to be true.

Mum and I had been exchanging frequent texts over the past twenty-four hours.

Any worries will go A&E. BUT not expecting worse. Sleep well and see you all tomorrow.

Despite having thrown the term around, I had to look it up when she told me about Dad's leg. DVT: deep vein thrombosis. Thrombosis: blood clot. Deep vein: veins deep in the body. I read: *Deep vein thrombosis can be serious because blood clots in your veins can break loose, travel through your bloodstream and lodge in your lungs, blocking blood flow (pulmonary embolism).* I read:

A pulmonary embolism can be life-threatening.

My father had a pulled muscle in his leg that wouldn't heal and after a car trip from Auckland it had become red, hot and painful. On Friday he'd had a blood test that came back positive for DVT, but he had to wait until after the long weekend for the decisive scan that would tell us how bad it was. His doctor had prescribed blood thinners to 'hold' it.

While the rest of us put on togs, he sat at the desk in the living room looking at calendars.

'We'll have to cancel that one, Gin,' he called out.

'What?' My mother was halfway down the stairs, tying a sarong over her swimsuit.

'The bike trip next month. Bloody pain.'

They had just got themselves electric bikes and were full of plans. Until now, car-free shopping missions had taken them around the windy harbour road on push bikes or on foot.

'Don't cancel it yet,' my mother said, leaning against his shoulder and looking down at the days ahead. There was an ease to how they inhabited space together, a routine developed over the sequence of houses they'd lived in since we'd all moved away, leaving the two of them alone for the first time in thirty years.

Dad said something I didn't hear, then stood and went to the other room, turning on the TV to the Australian Open. He had projects, he'd told us; there was an article about the policy implications of the popularity of SUVs in New Zealand, and jobs in the garden. He was also working on a novel, but he tended not to mention that. Right then, it was hard to settle to anything.

There wasn't much for it but to head down to the sea without him, the girls on their scooters shooting way ahead of Tim, Mum and me. Just before the Pavilion café in Days Bay, they dropped their scooters to climb up the bank and down the other side, emerging grubby with dirt. It was crowded down there by the beach. We paused in front of the new information panels with their photographs of Katherine Mansfield – she had spent her summers in the eastern bays, and set some of her stories here – and ghostly early twentieth-century black-and-white images of day-trippers, who used to come here by ferry. This was once Wellington's answer to Coney Island, a seaside resort complete with Australasia's largest water shoot. It was also Oruamatoro, a pā site and kāinga. According to the panels, remnants of the walls from Māori gardens had been found behind the tennis courts. The panels didn't say how one place had become another.

Swimming had always been more Mum's thing than Dad's. It was her I'd followed in my determination not to become the kind of woman who worried about getting salt and chlorine in her hair. Perhaps Mum was reacting against her own mother's advice that a married woman should put on her makeup before breakfast. Anyway, she was always in the water with us, while Dad's swims were more intermittent.

As we crossed the road to the beach, though, I remembered Dad jumping off the ferry wharf with us earlier in the summer, a man of seventy-five claiming his turn among a bunch of shoving teenage boys and young men. And jumping with him, the rest of us – his daughter, now a woman in her forties, and his granddaughters, two nine-year-old girls.

Today, in the late afternoon heat, the beach was packed. Groups of boys in board shorts and picnicking families in long-sleeved togs were all crowded together, and as always lots of grandparents were on duty. Lena and Natasha, their goggles on before the rest of us reached the sand, were knee-deep in the water. That long curve of sea and sand was one of the places they belonged. It was far warmer than on our side of the city, protected in the layered embrace of hills.

While the girls dived and splashed, Mum, Tim and I settled on towels, Tim into reading, and Mum and I into talk, as usual, about my brothers and cousins – so many cousins. She had had sixty of them, but fewer every year. I still had thirty. Our girls had three. It was like an exaggerated chart of the shift in family size over three generations.

'I'm worried about the leg,' she said.

His breath had been short that morning.

We talked about what could happen, but what was there to say about uncertainty?

As I often did around that time, I felt glad of my two brothers, neither of whom we'd yet told. They were both a long way away – Medellín and Perth – but I was still grateful we'd be in the next phase together.

Mum and I talked, instead, about the family Christmas we'd just had. Everyone seemed to have brought a beast from whatever piece of land they came from. 'Who will support us farmers?' one uncle only half joked as we pushed our vegetarian sausages and corn onto one side of the barbecue.

I hadn't mentioned that we were now also trying to cut down on dairy – I wasn't up for that kind of confrontation at a family Christmas. Besides, what language would we have for it? Our talk was bred on a chatty jokiness through which we sometimes managed to pass affection over quite vast distances in imaginings of the world. My mother had been the butt of jokes about 'you greenies' for years, although not so much from my own generation of cousins. I'd been due on election day 1975, when she was a candidate for the Values Party, predecessors to the Greens.

We talked about what was happening with the skate park she'd been trying to help get up and running as part of her role on the community board, and the opposition of some of the older locals. The intense and widely reported generational debate surrounding the park made it sound as though the people opposed to it thought the 'youths' it might attract spent their time taking drugs and having sex, with a preference for public places.

And we talked about the proposed walking and cycling path to Petone, another of Mum's concerns, and how it had finally been approved by the wider council. The path was designed in part to help future-proof the road with a strengthened sea wall. When seas were high, storm surges could hurl water and rocks across the road and sometimes pull chunks of asphalt back in. Mum and Dad could get cut off out there. Many of the seaside houses could no longer get insurance; it wouldn't take much sea rise to compromise them.

We stuck to the pitch of a family conversation. We didn't talk about Trump. We'd talked enough about Trump. And Brexit. We didn't even talk (much) about climate change. There was nothing we could do about my father but wait.

It hadn't always been this easy with my parents – it wasn't always, even now – but over the past few years, or since our children were born, a tension had fallen away.

My mother had started talking recently about my and my brothers' childhoods, and about her own, swimming with her five siblings in the Hutt River not far away, and at Raumati on the coast, where I'd been recently. And of summers with her grandparents and cousins on their farm. Or perhaps I had only just started listening.

There on the beach, I was the first adult to get in. The kids and I had developed a ritual that summer in which they counted me down. Ten, nine, eight. I watched the waves. Seven, six, five, four. I was waist-deep now. This standing, watching, half in, half out is part of the pleasure of swimming. Three, two, one – and I was in, diving and staying under long enough for the cool to pass right through and become part of my body. The water of my body contained within the water of the sea. The water of a world beyond me.

The girls took my hands and led me to an undersea garden they were creating, diving down to place stones in a circle around a starfish. I blinked against the salty water, letting Lena guide my fingers to the sandpaper skin of the starfish floating gently just above the sand, rocking with each wave. Out there, treading water, I became aware of my mother on the beach watching. Conscious of her seeing me being a mother. Of her seeing these children we had all made. I felt almost painfully in the midst of life then, fully daughter and mother all at once, full of the stretch of a human life and the fierce pleasure of it. Of its beauty and its passing.

When my mother and Tim joined us, they each took a turn of the offered starfish, before returning it to sway down slowly to the sea floor.

Although it wasn't unusual for my father not to be here in these swims, his absence moved with us, a tight pull like water roped around our legs.

Later, back up at the house and showered free of salt – Lena, Natasha and me in pyjamas – we ate Mum's chickpea soup for dinner. I read to the girls, one daughter leaning into each side of me on the sofa, leaving Tim to talk and help with the dishes.

My father loved talking with him, often saying, 'Actually, this would interest Tim . . .'

His belief in what would interest the father of his grandchildren was endless – endless to the point where I sometimes wanted to say, it might interest your daughter too. It reminded me of his father, my grandfather, and how, when we went around to visit, he always had a news clipping or two that might 'interest us'. Of course, inevitably, I wished I had paid more attention to that too.

After the girls were in bed and we were heading that way as well, my parents were briefly tempted again to the tennis. From our bedroom we could hear the grunts of the new young star taking on the veteran, the two men almost a generation apart. I heard Dad saying to my mother, 'It has all the elements of a Greek drama.'

When I woke in the night to the sound of a ruru, and what I thought was the sea but was just a breeze in the trees, the house felt full, hot with pairs of sleepers: Lena and Natasha in their twin beds in the back room, Tim and me in the middle room that hangs as a loft out above the living area, and my parents in their bedroom, the only room with a view of the sea. I thought of that starfish, drifting in its garden on the sea floor, while around us the house itself became a kind of ark, floating us through a darkness as thick as blood. I wondered if Dad would be the first up as usual. Or if tomorrow would be the day that was different.

'Hello, you two little sillies. What time did you wake up?'

My mother. Still in bed. I could hear the sleepiness in her voice.

'Six thirty-three.'

I thought that was Lena. My twins' voices are the hardest thing to tell apart.

'*I* woke first. I woke at six twenty-five.'

That was definitely Natasha. Even more precise than her sister. We'd taught them not to disturb us until seven, and they were good at staying in bed and reading. This was no longer new, but it was still a pleasure, the fact they were capable of taking themselves silently off into their own stories.

'Pretty good,' said my mother. 'Shall we let Mum and Dad sleep?'

They'd need a bigger house for that, but I appreciated the gesture. Tim was still managing to doze beside me, his breath regular and deep, the warmth of his body close in the small bed I had slept in alone for years as a teenager when we lived on the Wairarapa farm.

Mum again. 'Are you going to snuggle in with me? Or go downstairs and help Grandpa with the porridge?'

So he was down there.

He didn't sleep much anymore, often waking at five, as his father had.

I heard the girls creep noisily down the hallway, past our room and down the stairs, which they treated as a slide. Then I could no longer hear words, just their voices mingling with my father's deeper tones, sounding as though he was being a monster for them, leaning over his cauldron of porridge, which they always say is better than the porridge I make. I lay there in the cocoon of the bed, picturing the three of them down there moving around in the morning kitchen, and my mother in the next room reading.

When we went for a bush walk around Lake Taupō at Christmas, Dad had claimed that the cold of the lake did wonders for his leg, which was already an issue. Now I wondered. At the time we were more worried about Mum's arthritic hip, managed by a daily dose of 100mg of Voltaren. She'd told me a standard tablet is 12.5mg. In a few weeks she would have a blood test to see how her kidneys were handling this; we didn't know it yet, but the answer would be, not well. Without this dose of pain relief and anti-inflammatories, it would be hard for her to walk from the house to the beach. I'd not yet seen this and still didn't fully believe it.

But at Christmas, as we picked our way around the slippery submerged rocks along the lakeshore, the girls leaping ahead with Tim, me hanging back with my parents, I was beginning to sense that I would eventually become more anxious about my parents than about my children. And that this would be a geological shift.

Then again, after Christmas, the two of them had gone for two weeks to Great Barrier Island, the original swimming place for me, where they stayed in the hut my father had built four decades earlier among ten acres of precipitous native bush. They bought the section, which had a clear cold stream running through it, when my mother was pregnant with me and she couldn't get down the steep slope into the bush. Sure, there's a flat area, my father had told her. Over the years they'd dug out enough of the slope to fit a tent, a small wooden table, stools, and two deck chairs so they could lie back and watch flights of kākā. On summer trips there as kids, the first job was digging the long-drop for the year. Recently, in a small concession to age, Dad constructed a proper long-drop on the site, with a seat and a roof, and put in a small rainwater tank so they didn't have to go way down to the stream for drinking water or to do dishes and washing. This was still their idea of a perfect holiday. When I turned forty, and my mother seventy, we got matching pōhutukawa tattoos. I was thinking of Great Barrier when I proposed it, only afterwards seeing how close it came to a rose tattoo, or the classic *I LOVE MUM*.

Lying in bed, I thought of last summer, when Tim and I took the kids to the Barrier for a week, the four of us sleeping at the tent site just up from the hut where my parents slept, and how stupid it seemed not to have found the time to make it over this year.

After another day at the beach, all of us there except Dad, Tim drove back home around the harbour so he could go to work the next day and I stayed on. None of us could quite imagine how it would work if I left the girls with them and Dad needed to go to the hospital in the night. My father, of course, told us not to be so ridiculous. I was staying not to look after my parents, but in case they couldn't look after my children. I felt like a linchpin between generations, holding the whole thing together.

Besides, it was still sometimes easier, more restful, to spend time with my parents without Tim, even after seventeen years – still that different ease with one's birth family. Or perhaps it was just that I still took a child's pleasure in getting my parents' attention to myself.

In the evening Fat Freddy's Drop was playing in the park by the beach, and the bass reached us on the still air. Tim and I had seen them in Berlin once, in the mid-2000s, at one of the trendy beach bars along the river. Now one of the band members was a bus-stop parent like us. We sometimes saw him, a handsome, quiet presence, standing off to the side of the cluster of chatting mothers in brightly coloured skirts, of which I was sometimes one, our days structured by our children's arrival home from school.

We walked up to a friend's house, where the view from the deck was like stadium seating for the gig. Lena and Natasha quickly formed a children's republic with the other kids, rampaging loudly off into the garden. My father, not seeming quite on for company, took me on a walk further up the road. We stood looking out over the body of the bay, the bush, the deep blue of the water with the wharf strung out into it, music drifting.

'God, it's beautiful here,' my father said.

They'd lived in this place longer than they had anywhere else. Before this, it was always a move every six years or so. Here, it seemed they had found a harbour.

When we got back to the gathering, however, there had been a drama. The four children had been caught slashing the tops off agapanthus and using them as guns. The other mother had gone to sort them out and I didn't think much of it, reasoning comfortably that my girls were unlikely to have been the instigators.

Half an hour later I went into the house to find everyone standing around awkwardly, Lena, in particular, stiff and strained.

She moved over to me quickly and took my hand. 'Can we go?'

I realised I hadn't got it. I hadn't understood.

I'd been digging up agapanthus at home the day before. Lena and Natasha were chatting to me while I hacked at the plants with the spade and pulled at their thick, tuber-like roots. A kererū had dive-bombed past on its way to the pūriri while we worked. The girls had helped me load the deep blue star flowers into a skip. Why wouldn't they have followed suit here, hacking off the heads, already imagining something new in their place?

'We're so sorry,' I said to the other mother. '*I'm* sorry.'

This was a beloved garden, the house up for sale next week so that the friends, the same age as my parents, could downsize, something my parents talked about doing too. Everything was in full, final bloom.

I took the hands of my now quiet daughters and we picked our way back along the path.

When one of the other girls came up with her parents to leave, and to apologise to her grandmother on the way, she was crying so much she could hardly breathe. Something had pulled loose.

I watched the grandmother leaning into the car, hugging the girl and saying, 'It's okay, it's okay, love. I know you're sorry. I know you didn't mean it.'

There seemed to be no anger in her, only sadness, the desire of an adult to comfort a child. Also a yearning of deep separation, of hurt she wanted to stop but couldn't. These children would remember things that would outlast us all.

On the walk home, Lena pulled at me and dissolved into tears. Her guilt tended to be at a higher pitch than her sister's, who wasn't so susceptible to feeling 'bad'.

'She loves her garden,' my father said.

'We didn't know,' Natasha responded quietly, almost stubbornly, dropping back slightly to walk beside my mother.

We all felt the shock of it, the child's shame at having got it wrong.

But what my father said was, 'Come on, Lena, it's not *so* terrible. Toughen up, girl.'

It was a joking effort to displace sadness, a familiar one to me. It didn't always leave much room to manoeuvre.

But he also put his arm awkwardly around her. He's a tall man. It contained the ghosting of an arm around me too as I continued to hold my daughter's hand.

'We didn't know where you were, Mum. We didn't know what to do.'

The following morning, while we waited for my father's hospital appointment and scan, he and I walked down the road for a coffee. I consciously adjusted my pace.

Dad looked tired, but he was still straight into it, into what he'd been reading. This time it was *A Stranger in the House*. He'd been thinking about his own family and about the war. He hadn't known his father, who was married in uniform, until he was two. He told me again the story of his first memory, of a stranger rolling a carpet-bag towards him and his mother at the train station. This was now seventy-three years ago. The book, he told me, was about the effects of war on the families and children of soldiers, and on how war impacts subsequent generations. All those men coming home with such experiences, most of which they didn't talk about. The other men in my grandfather's wedding party died – brother, new brother-in-law, best friends. My father had been thinking about his relationship with his father and how hard it had sometimes been to be close.

I ended up talking, in return, about what I was trying to write, and the sometimes troubling way it pulled other people in. This felt connected in some way not only to how we create characters from real people in non-fiction, but also to how we imagine the people in our lives. Especially family. 'We use our parents like recurring dreams,' Doris Lessing wrote in a piece about her father, 'to be entered into when needed.' We do so much work on the people around us, even after they are gone. Family is so much a part of how I measured my place in the world.

I wished we could have talked forever. It was becoming clear we could have new conversations at every stage.

When we walked back up to the house, I noticed my parents'

latest bumper sticker. They've always had bumper stickers. Our 1970s red station wagon, in which as kids we sometimes shared the boot with the CNG tank, was festooned with them: *Friends of the Earth, Save Aramoana, Nuke Free, Values.* They've had *Stop the Tour, Support the Homosexual Law Reform Bill,* and *Go Green.* But their new bumper sticker was in support of *End-of-Life Choice (Fewer will Suffer).*

My father was big on this bill, although he hadn't talked about it much. It was my mother who insisted I read Atul Gawande's *Being Mortal,* which helped me understand that no one is really 'young' in their seventies. The story of ageing, Gawande writes, is the story of our parts. Things fall apart. Perhaps the bumper sticker was a claim on dignity, a claim to wanting to approach that last thing on their own terms. But there was a confronting baldness to it.

When Mum got back, she and Dad drove away to the hospital for the scan. The girls and I walked to the sea to swim again, which I needed now perhaps more than my children. It was breezy down there, the water churned up, green with roiling sand.

Afterwards, the house felt empty and quiet. I noticed the whirr of the late summer cicadas, humming in the heat while the three of us lay on the concrete in our togs trying to warm up.

On the grass in the back garden, we ate a lunch of sweetcorn and boiled eggs and carrots, crunching lettuce from Dad's vege patch.

I'm not sure the girls knew we were waiting.

While I tried to catch up on work, rewriting a syllabus for the coming teaching semester, they created a café menu. The café games had intensified and become more sophisticated since they'd come to understand that their uncle ran a real restaurant in Colombia. Their café was called 'The Healthy Carrot'; I chose the tomato salad from the formally presented menu and received a whole tomato served on a small plastic plate with a miniature plastic knife and fork. It made me feel like an awkward, oversized child, playing at being the oldest in the place. My heart creaked at the thought I would be.

Finally, the phone rang.

'It's fine,' my mother said. 'He's fine. There's nothing there.'

The breath caught in my lungs.

Only when my parents arrived back half an hour later did I realise fully how strained they'd been, how anxious. Their faces had changed colour as though blood was moving freely again, pumping through reopened veins.

With a returned lightness, free to leave my parents and children together again, I hugged everyone goodbye and caught the next ferry into the city and home. Before I left, Dad said that when they came to drop the kids off he could bring his chainsaw over and chop up a fallen tree for firewood. They were back.

In the evening, Mum texted to say she'd been reading the girls versions of Shakespeare stories she read me as a kid.

Have read Shrew in Seraillier version. Tasha very keen for more so had Lear (eye gouging left out) tonight. Both feeling new life!

And the next day.

Happy day. Picnic in park, now to swim in wind.

I imagined them out there together, my father in the water this time too, wind flicking froth off the waves high into the air, slick silver kahawai slipping across the ocean floor.

The Whale

Friday 29 June, 2018
We drive down to the south coast in the bright sun after school and my daughters climb the rocks with me trailing close behind. Often I don't follow, but today I choose to.

The waves are huge gentle things, rising in slopes before falling sumptuously back. In their sneakers and warm coats, the children pick their way out along the sharp rocks, shouting TSUNAMI ALERT each time an especially big wave rolls in.

Since the 2016 earthquakes it has become easier to imagine the movements that pushed these rocks out of the sea. The Kaikōura ranges too, a spine against the sky that feels dynamic, pushing upwards. Earth in motion. Today, the ranges' snow-white tips cast cold onto the crests of the waves, and there's a blast from the south, where there's only sea until Antarctica.

At the highest places, tiny taupata trees try to grow in crevices. The girls have specific plants they want to show me, miniature plantations. We go out to the furthest point where waves froth white, refreshing galaxies of rock pools.

On our way back to the car I walk ahead and when I look back my children are standing on top of a rock; they too have become silhouettes reaching into the deepening sky, each of them a minor mountain.

Tuesday 3 July

Before school drop-off and work we get down to Princess Bay again. The blue-green waves rush in under a dark purple sky. Natasha shouts into the wind. Further around the coast on Te Raekaihau Point, people arrive in orange high-vis vests and kneel down to plant grasses and flax.

Later in the day I go for a run alone out along from the west arm of Lyall Bay. Kite surfers are on the water, each one first wrestling strips of coloured nylon on the beach, then they're off, their half-moon sails moving in arcs. I watch and run and breathe while a small human figure in parallel to me but on the water holds the wind steady, kite moving at a 45-degree angle against the air. In the moment I turn away and then back, they too have flipped the sail and are moving at speed, flying high over waves. Sails leap across the bay like dolphins.

Thursday 5 July

Tim's away and Lena's home sick. Yesterday we hardly moved from the sofa so we didn't see the sea. Our world contracts to the living-room fire, *Danger Mouse* on YouTube for Lena, video meetings with students for me.

At our kitchen table, we watch clips of a southern right whale that has arrived in Wellington Harbour, its slow movements just reaching through the water's surface.

A whale was last seen in the harbour in 2010. This floats a story of hope. Southern right whales were hunted almost to extinction in the eighteenth and nineteenth centuries. Their population may have dropped as low as a hundred at one point. Sightings are slowly returning. On my Facebook feed, an older man posts about the harbour when he was young. He says whales wouldn't have gone near that filth. When orca visit, as they sometimes do now, such visitations are taken as signs of the water's health. It seems to me that's what we want to believe.

Lena and I drive down to the beachside café near the airport so we can watch the planes. The whale is there on the front page of the newspaper. Beside me, Lena draws a picture in her book with the title 'Southern right whale in Wellington harbour'. She puts a thought bubble above its head saying, RARE. The strangeness of the whale's head in the newspaper photo, which looks as much rock as beast, is transmuted into a smiley creature in her drawing: friendly, cheerful. The familiarity of the metamorphosis makes me laugh.

Outside, sun through the clouds makes the wave crests gleam white as they break. Far out, the Interislander ferry heads south. A small NZ Post truck drives past with mail from the airport.

The everyday of this coast isn't stationary, I remember; it isn't just about rocks. It's about being on the edge of the sea, about shipping lines and flight paths and whale migration routes. Though it is also, right here in rocky, chilly juttings, the edge of an island pushed up from beneath.

I find I'm thinking about Charlotte Smith, whose work I teach, and her two-hundred-year-old poems of the rocky Sussex coast, which have often been with me since I edited them. She stood on her own rocky shore watching trading ships and birds appearing on the horizon from elsewhere. I think, too, of a description from Mary Wollstonecraft's travel book about journeying around the Scandinavian coastline with her baby daughter in 1795 – coastal rocks as 'the bones of the world'.

Back at home, for something closer to this place, I dig out a recent essay-poem by Kāpiti Coast writer Lynn Jenner and read of the sound of waves 'arriving from thousands of miles away. / By the time news from the rest of the world arrives here its voice is faint and barely audible above the noise of these waves.'

Nonetheless, it arrives.

*

I read hourly updates on the boys trapped in the Thai cave. At first it seemed they would just disappear and become one of those stories – the children who were taken by water. But now they've been located. Back on our sofa we stream the video of the diver who found them.

'We come, we come,' he keeps saying.

He sounds like a British friend of ours, his voice echoing with an uncanny familiarity in the watery cave through the bubbles of his air tank. The torch pans over the figures, counting them.

'Where you come from?' The boys this time.

'England, the UK.' His voice sounds hollow.

Lena and I watch the video again and again, in all its strangeness. The boys look like kids excited about being on film, crouched on the cave floor with their legs pulled up. After nine days underground in the cave trapped by surprise movements of the sea, they're still wearing red soccer outfits.

There are reports of a storm coming and they need to teach these boys, who are between eleven and sixteen and who can't swim, to scuba dive. There is a choice – to risk them being drowned by rising water when the monsoon rains arrive, or to risk making a rescue attempt.

Friday 6 July
Lena's back at school and after a morning's work I drive into the city and down to the harbour with my friend S. I'm light with the breathing space of having gone very part-time at work, having felt a rising need to decompress for, well, perhaps since I returned to full-time teaching with two one-year-olds, beginning years of rushing between one thing and another. It's a break to pause and take stock.

We end up parked by the railway station, and it's hard to get to the water past the ferry terminal. We walk beside wire fences along an industrial part of the wharf I've never been on before. It smells, but not like big business, more like oil and fish. The boats docked here are small and dirty, their boards old.

Down the end of the wharf there's a man looking out – or rather looking into his phone. He tells us the whale was spotted near the Interislander ferry terminal thirty minutes ago, stopping the ferry from docking.

We look hopefully at the dappled sea.

S. tells me about a link on Facebook shared by another friend, K., about how there were once so many whales in the harbour there are spots named for whale watching. The whale is remaking the memory of the place.

We've heard she may be here to calve. Further up the coast South Taranaki Bight was once known as Mothering Bay, because of all the southern rights who used to go there to give birth.

I make bad jokes about baby prime ministers and baby whales, remembering the night a few weeks ago when Jacinda had her baby. Like everyone else it seems, I can't help investing that birth with symbolism. As the news came in of our prime minister in labour, Tim and I and the girls were standing in a crowd at a winter solstice festival, watching an enormous, papier-mâché figure burn on a raft on Whairepo Lagoon in central Wellington. As the figure flamed orange on the dark water, a woman spoke through a loudspeaker about the fear we feel for this planet, and of a curse by which we may have made it forever cold. And of the need to burn the old year away. For a moment we stood fleetingly together in the lit-up night in some kind of hope for a change in the seasons.

S. and I don't see the whale but when I take the long route home along the harbour for school pick-up, the water's scalloped surface looks either empty or full of potential, barely a skein across an unseen aspect of the world.

Water is where the other world seems to live – the world beyond the human. I think of Pip Adam's *The New Animals* as I drive, and the way the long, strange swim at the end of that novel, in which a human character metamorphoses (back) into something other than (more than?) human, has helped to make a briny underwater ecology present to me. That entrance and awakening of a space in the imagination stories can create.

At school it's pyjama day to celebrate the end of term, and the girls are giddy, coming at me with piles of art to thrust into my hands before running off with friends. Among the parents, all talk is of the whale. She's made us a small town, filled with gossip about the arrival of a stranger. The new story is she's here to find a mate. It's a more melancholy story than the birthing one, suggesting need rather than abundance.

One mother saw her today and heard the ferry honking. 'I mean, what did they expect?' she says. 'Acknowledgement she was in a place reserved for human business? It was pretty crazy.' She laughs and hands around her phone with a photo. In the other part of her life she's a doctor.

On my own phone news alerts start coming through about the Thai boys. A former Thai Navy SEAL has died during an operation to install air tanks in the cave. I want to remember his name. Saman Kunan. He swam through the tunnels to the boys to deliver oxygen, but in the end didn't have enough to get himself back. He lost consciousness as he left the cave complex, caught in the wrong element.

While my children swing upside down from monkey bars, cartoon-coloured in their winter onesies, I look at a photo of three boys. They're wrapped in clear plastic raincoats thin as cellophane.

Saturday 7 July
We're now calling the whale Matariki, and she's taken on the

mythical characteristics of a visitor of the Māori New Year, which I've begun to pay proper attention to this year mainly because the kids are learning about it at school. The appearance of the Matariki star cluster in midwinter begins a period of celebration and renewal. Matariki fireworks in the harbour have been postponed; we can't blast this creature from our harbour. There is pleasure in being made to adjust.

In order to relieve congestion in troublesome places, the council has issued advice about where to go to see the whale. Before we leave the house, I stand at the door shouting at Lena and Natasha about choices, and how they seem to be choosing putting on their shoes over seeing a whale.

'Come *on*,' I say.

'We're *doing* it,' they shout back, shoes no closer to being on. At least they've moved on from kicking each other.

The noise is doing my head in. We're squeezing the viewing in between morning toast and picking Tim up from the airport. I remind myself Lena is still exhausted and irritable from her flu, which had her shaking wet with sweat in my bed not so many nights ago.

It's raining too, but we drive to Wadestown anyway, park on the curb, and join the crowd waiting on the footpath.

Light rain slicks up my glasses and I am busy adjusting Lena's and Natasha's raincoat zips when it first surfaces, a grey head appearing with surprising buoyancy from the choppy waves. Then the whale is on her back, wallowing and sticking out in two places a startling distance from each other.

We watch as she turns on her head, swimming under the water, flinging her tail in the air and thumping it down hard.

Lena's and Natasha's small faces are lit with it, pink and wet in the cold.

She is enormous.

I turn back and forth from the whale to the rare sight of my silenced children.

Wednesday 11 July

In a Mojo café, two bearded men at a table near me talk, one in heavy-rimmed glasses, the other with a European or South American accent. The one with the more substantial beard is talking rapidly. 'We can't fix anything with this concept of ownership in place,' he says. 'There's no hope for sustainability when people always have a structure of gain. We need a new ecosystem.' He speaks in full paragraphs. Astonishingly, it seems like a job interview, or at least a networking conversation. The man with the accent says he'll need a little longer to think through these ideas.

Friday 13 July

The boys in the cave have been pushed unconscious through a kilometre of submerged rock passages to the open air. Every one of them. Elon Musk showed up 'on location' with an impractical kid-sized mini-submarine and got aggressive when he was told it wouldn't help. The rescue was done by divers, each holding a sedated child to his chest, a small human package breathing visible bubbles of life into the water.

The whale's moved too, first spending time near Hataitai and the airport, then finding her way to the harbour mouth and setting out into the sea.

Last night in a bar in town, Tim and I talked with friends about whether people had seen the whale. One friend told us about being in the lunchroom at work, feeling stressed over another restructure, and being told by a colleague, 'Go out and see the whale. If you feel nothing and are still stressed, then you need help.' It sounded like a belief in nature as cure brought into the city. A belief that spending time in the company of the non-human world – in the bush, or with other creatures – can make us feel better. It's not that I don't believe this. I think I do. Only it seems like a limited kind of imagining – a whale appearing here for our benefit.

Earlier in the week I heard a woman talking on the radio about where Matariki might head next, potentially to the known winter spot for southern rights in a marine mammal sanctuary off Taranaki. The sanctuary is also home to the critically endangered Māui dolphin, she said, and the government has just granted a seabed mining exploration permit within the area.

Sentimentality, and some vague feeling that we *need* these creatures, doesn't seem to get us very far towards recognition of their own subjectivities and needs, or of the ecologies they depend on to survive.

There was something in the whale's presence in our human harbour that demanded: *Look. This is what I am. Pay attention.*

Saturday 14 July
We watch the postponed Matariki fireworks from a distance, sitting on the Tomb of the Unknown Warrior at Pukeahu Park and looking up at the explosions of coloured fire above the harbour. The whale still feels present, the subject of swapped fragments of conversation between strangers. A group near us talk about the recent shift of the annual city fireworks from Guy Fawkes to midwinter Matariki, wondering why it took so long, the late, light evenings of November never working for fireworks in our hemisphere. The cold, lit-up dark feels right, the city re-centred around the bowl of its harbour, leaning in to this Indigenous solstice.

Sunday 15 July
In the morning the four of us drive down to Lyall Bay before seven to try to see the Matariki sky, and the stars the girls' teachers have told them are best seen just before dawn. By the time we get there,

we're too late for stars, but not too late to watch the dim but already gleaming sea turning from darkness to light. As the tide pulls the water in, the waves are hardly more than breaths in the morning air. Natasha leaps along the beach, grabbing my hand to walk out onto the small concrete wharf. The sea moves up either side of us until we could be standing on the prow of a ship. Slowly the sea turns orange.

Thursday 19 July

School holidays. Tim's on duty today and I decide to cross the harbour and spend time in the quiet of my parents' house in Days Bay while they're away. Alone this time, I bike down to the harbour ferry. The water turns grey and deep, now moving in raised hills but not with the orderly rhythm of shore-bound waves. Out here it's more chaotic, its direction unclear.

A friend told me recently about how the harbour was once filled with waka, a highway rather than a gap to be driven around.

As the ferry motors on, I read on my phone it looks like Matariki is a male whale after all. They – the scientists and whale experts – can't be certain until they've done DNA tests from a dart fired into its skin. In the news reports he's called a taonga.

The need to decide on the gender of the whale, the tohorā, feels strange. Perhaps the whale could be a 'they' to us, as it would be in te reo Māori? Ia.

Only fifteen minutes from shore, once the ferry is further out almost at Matiu/Somes Island – former pā site, former prisoner-of-war camp, former quarantine station, now Department of Conservation reserve – I can see through the headlands to the ocean, the frame of hills disappearing into the sea. Tim and I camped on the island for a friend's fortieth a few months ago, walking out drunk with torches and spotting a little blue penguin waddling in panic ahead of us, and a tuatara lying still across the path then darting away into the undergrowth. For a fleeting moment in the torchlight the tuatara, with its scaly green-grey folds of skin, spiny back, and splayed lizard legs, looked like the living dinosaur it was.

The next morning, a delayed ferry had made us feel far from shore. Water makes distance feel further than it does across land.

Out on the water again I'm tempted to romanticise, to imagine the whale paying homage to the taniwha Whātaitai, who according to the story was stranded there on the isthmus after trying to follow his brother, Ngake, into the open sea.

The ferry pushes on.

Wednesday 25 July
When school starts again it turns us back towards the south coast. I meant to reconfigure my attention from land to sea this month. Now, for the moment at least, I feel us not as hillside suburbs connected by road-veined valleys, but as an island within water.

Thursday 26 July
I finally walk to school with the girls. It's the first time in July. Tim goes to work early, and there's the usual slight skirmish around getting lunches made and bags packed, but then we're out in the wet grass, turned luminous green in the fleeting sun as we cross the field. Natasha, still carrying some unnamed fury from the tussle of getting out of the house, waves a short stick and keeps hitting me and Lena (by *accident*) until I make her throw it away. Then I grab her and tell her to pause, breathe, look at that tree. Its trunk is stripped bare, a clean and beautiful eucalyptus. The tree's not angry, I say. *I'm* not angry (although I sometimes am). I don't say that second bit. Further on, our eyes are drawn up and across the water to the Kaikōura ranges. They're thick with white now, even on the closer peaks. The sky has turned purple and rain begins to spit. Even then, I love that we can walk together looking

directly south at the generous opening out of the sea.

As we cross the road and start on down the long winding footpath through the trees to the school, Lena tells me she and Natasha have paid the taniwha – by which she means the sealed path – so that one human at a time can walk along its long back. They have bought me passage, breaking our fates free of the constraints of realism or strict time. They dip and dance, gathering grass, pointing out horses, skipping way ahead and greeting school friends who appear from tributary paths, a flotilla of primary school kids flowing down the hill, making up the world as they go. While we walk, I am right there, in the awakening morning.

Friday 27 July
Shouldn't I swim? It looks so cold. Besides, actually swimming feels like taking this whole water business a bit too literally.

Monday 6 August
In the zoo café I run into a new artist friend, A. She is here to think about the whakapapa and genealogy of animals. She's interested in how diverse connections show whakapapa is not linear but genealogical, reaching out in multiple directions. A. is writing about the whale, making a piece for Matariki celebrations next year.

I show her the 'waterlog' I kept over the month of July and she talks in response about an exhibition she did for the Common Ground Festival in Lower Hutt. She has a walking art practice. In this piece she took people walking beside water. The piece was to be on the Waiwhetū Stream, she says, but in the end she had come to understand there were three bodies of water – the stream, the aquifer, and the sea. She tells me about how water has different guardians in kaupapa Māori understanding depending on its state – rain in the sky, river in the streams in the land, and then there is the sea. They each have their own gods and names.

There is a pause when A. stops talking about the Common Ground project. Then she says, but there are also so many English understandings of water.

English. I haven't been thinking of my own understandings that way and feel joltingly bereft, adrift in place. In search of something to say, I start talking about *Moby Dick* – after all I'm meant to be a literary scholar – but this makes me feel sadder still, thinking of that book with its astonishing sentences and evocation of a world of water, but which is also a saga of hunting whales and boiling them down for oil, bone and meat. I didn't even finish it.

I want ways of understanding to be in conversation with one another, so that I can learn from without claiming ownership of stories different from my own. Ways to inhabit this place as Pākehā, to acknowledge Māori as Indigenous, without placing myself at an unswimmable remove. I sense I need also to continue feeling the discomfort integral to these imaginings of how to belong.

I find I start, instead of talking about *Moby Dick*, to talk with her about how my family stood in our coats in the rain and watched the whale's magnificent tail flick.

But where's the sense of history in that?

A. says that for her, the visit of this whale, this tohorā, is a visit from an ancestor, a tipuna. It's like a new myth, like the visit of the whale ridden by Ngāti Porou and Ngāi Tahu ancestor Paikea.

We need some new myths.

Before she leaves she tells me she's going to the zoo. She could stand in front of the tuatara forever, she says.

Once she's gone, I'm left wondering if the whale seemed to carry stories because they visited us while we stayed in place, so their narratives and ours spilled into one another.

In the news today there's another image of the Thai boys. They have been transformed from small soccer players into trainee

Buddhist novices, preparing to live in a temple for nine days to give thanks, and to honour those who rescued them. I wonder how the parents can let them go so soon. Each child is shaven-headed, a red robe off each shoulder. Some of them are stateless, with no country to which they belong. They look like children who have passed through water and arrived home from another realm, but carrying it with them.

Swimming Out

Medellín

My brother told us the bad news before we left the airport terminal. Someone had vomited in the apartment pool. This being Colombia, it was unlikely to be sorted quickly.

I saw Lena and Natasha deflate slightly. This was part of how we'd pitched the trip to them: the first place we'd stay would be in an apartment in the hills and there would be a pool. They were nine and it had seemed the right way to ease in, give ourselves space to settle, get over jet lag, get used to being somewhere we didn't speak the language – it would be a bubble between us and the city, and perhaps travel itself. Besides, my brother Tom – who had become Tomas here in Colombia – said it was very Medellín to live in an apartment complex, at least for the new middle classes.

When I hugged him at the arrival gate I felt how skinny his shoulders had become. He'd visited us a couple of times in the past few years, but I'd only been here once, for three days six years ago on my way back from a work trip to somewhere else. Medellín was a complicated and expensive destination to get to, placing him even further away from us than it seemed on a map.

This time it felt as though I'd delivered a present.

Look. Finally. I brought the family. Like I promised.

I'd grown increasingly uninterested, anyway, in solitary journeys. That was only one of the ways to move – both at home and overseas – despite being the one that still took up so much of our collective imaginative space dedicated to 'travel'. Apart from a period as an exchange student in Japan, like many people my age my own early experiences of travel had been mostly a matter of Lonely Planet guides and single beds in youth hostel dormitories. Later, Tim and I travelled a bit together before our girls were born, but afterwards it was a few days here, a few days there, occasional longer solitary trips for work. My weird swimming expedition in 2017. This was our first attempt at a far-flung family journey.

Nearly twenty years ago I wrote a thesis about British family travel in the early tourist boom years of the nineteenth century, when the advent of trains and guidebooks and Thomas Cook tours made it possible for middle-class family groups to set off to 'see the world' – or, at least, see the seaside or a city in Europe. I knew that, from the outset, families on the move proved a convenient foil for those who wanted to conceive of themselves as proper travellers, in contrast to these naïve, bumbling (female) 'tourists', taking their homes (and children) along with them. It had always felt like a false split to me, but we'd also never really taken our children along with us before. Nor were we sure about the whole tourist endeavour – for anyone.

Anyway, we weren't really thinking of this as tourism yet. What we wanted was to visit my grown-up little brother, and the place he'd chosen to make a home. This had been on every 'list for the future' Tim and I had made over the past few years. We'd been saving up since our girls started school. We all wanted to visit other lives.

So here we were.

Medellín is in a mountain valley in the northern Andes, its airport in the hills outside the city.

In the coming days we would ride the train beside the river and gondolas up the hillsides, but for now, it was all only shapes in the dark. Tom drove us down the steep road in a borrowed family car, pulling out of the busy traffic at one point to suggest we get out and look at the view. It was evidently the thing to do. Across the road, men and motorbikes gathered in groups on the grassy curb while other motorbikes hurtled around the blind corner. In the valley beneath, a central stream of light mapped out the contours of the city, tributaries branching off up the seams of hillside gullies.

By the time we got to the neighbourhood of El Poblado, we'd been travelling for nearly twelve hours, starting in LA, where we'd swum with friends in the sea during an overnight stopover already a time zone away. We unloaded our backpacks and looked up at the building where we were to stay, thirty-two storeys high with its name flashing in white neon: The Ocean. Medellín is an hour's flight from both the Caribbean and the Pacific coasts; the majority of Colombians, my brother said, would never have seen the ocean. I tried to imagine that, and also what it was like for him living here, so far from the sea.

The apartment itself was like nowhere we'd ever stayed, the balcony with a view down the city's veins of light. Airbnb had only just taken off in Medellín, a city of 2.5 million, and the apartment had clearly been retrofitted for it, as many bedrooms as possible packed in and the paint fresh but thin.

Tom had bought us bread and eggs and avocados the size of small rugby balls. Lena and Natasha twirled on high stools at the breakfast bar while the kitchen got chaotic with a genuine midnight feast. Soon Tom was toasting bread on the stove and we were cracking open orange passionfruit and drinking mandarin juice. There were two kinds of nut butter made that morning by a friend of his who was trying to start a business.

The girls could be tricky to tell apart, especially if you didn't see them often, but Tom seemed to be getting the hang of it.

He had looked at them hard at the airport, grabbing a bright child's backpack in each hand. Lena declared she loved avocado and it was Lena who got the avocado toast, Natasha chocolate peanut butter. I gave Tom the hint it was most likely to be Lena if her blond-brown curls were tied up into a ponytail, Natasha if her hair was out – she liked wearing her curls loose in a way she described as 'wild'. After a day on a plane, this meant a messy mass. The girls were already talking to their uncle non-stop and would hardly take breath in the two weeks we were all together.

Because this is Medellín, *La Ciudad de la Eterna Primavera*, 'the city of eternal spring', and the temperature hovers constantly between around 17 and 27 degrees Celsius, the kitchen was open to the balcony, sliding doors and windows pushed right back. After their toast, the girls took fruit outside, standing close together and leaning over the balcony railing dripping juice, heads held close before the immensity of the city night. Floors below, but tantalisingly close, the pool jutting out from the building glowed aqua blue.

It was 1am when my brother left, heading back into the city to return the car he'd borrowed and then go to his one-bedroom apartment. He lived on the flat in the centre of El Poblado near Zorba, his café-restaurant where we'd head the next day. The girls' last question before sleep was whether they'd be able to swim in the morning.

In the following days, we checked the pool a number of times a day. Tim swotted up questions from our phrasebook to ask the revolving group of uniformed men downstairs. He'd done better at learning a smattering of Spanish than I had. We could never fully understand the answers, except the negative communicated by a shaken head and regretful tones.

The days were long. The best parts were at Zorba. The first morning we walked there and got lost even with my brother in the narrow winding streets. The steep footpath kept disappearing and half the time Tom had to walk on the road, jumping aside as cars and motorbikes and scooters shot by.

Zorba is on a quiet side street and that first morning we got there as staff were just starting to arrive, tables pushed back for cleaning. Tom introduced us then showed us the giant new pizza ovens they'd had installed in the kitchen since I was last here, and about which we'd received regular updates. He showed Lena and Natasha enormous blocks of mozzarella and rising pizza bases in the industrial-sized fridges around the brick walls. Then he had a plumber to talk with, so I led Tim and the girls downstairs to see the avocado tree in the garden and the hand-tiled basins in the bathrooms. Tom and his business partner, J., a skinny British vegan man, bought this as a derelict building at roughly the same time our daughters were born. They taught themselves demolition, construction, then how to cook and make coffee and drinks. Zorba is vegetarian, which they keep quiet in an effort not to scare off customers. It was all a story my family liked to tell.

Tim and I learnt different things in those years, I guess, although maybe demolition wasn't an inappropriate way to think about what the arrival of children does to lives. There was also something of construction, of making – first in and from our bodies, then a year of double breast-feeding, sometimes so deep in the night we heard the lions in the zoo start up their dawn roars. And something of rebuilding. We'd taught ourselves how to be parents, how to live our lives with and around our two small girls. It was a work in progress, freighted with everyday risk. After the intensity of the domestic years, this trip felt like a step into the next phase.

As I headed back up the stairs behind the girls and Tim, it felt almost as hard to remember Zorba hadn't always been part of my brother's life as that these three people, walking ahead of me, hadn't always been part of mine – I'd not always been a partner and a mother, not just daughter and sister. Tom wasn't always going to be this man running a café in Colombia.

It took a while that first morning, as things with Tom tend to. He got involved with making coffees for everyone – the plumber, the cleaner, then me and Tim. He made tall juices for the girls. He offered us breakfast dessert.

I kept thinking about the name: Zorba, from *Zorba the Greek* starring Anthony Quinn. It was one of my parents' favourite films and they showed it to Tom on a visit home while Zorba was being built but was still unnamed. At the end of the film, after a huge crash has destroyed their mad project and everything is lost, Zorba 'the Greek' persuades his uptight English boss, 'the writer' (who knows about life only through books), to dance with him amid the chaos on the beach. I was curious about why my parents, and now my brother, loved the film quite so much. It all seemed a bit romanticised and exoticised 1960s – it was certainly very male. Perhaps that was the point. But the awkward dance on the beach moved me too. *A man needs a little madness*, Zorba says, *to cut the rope and break free.*

The restaurant doubled as an art gallery and late in the evening a music venue, the tables pushed back for dancing. But I noted, too, that the slices of apple cake Tom served us were from a recipe of my mother's, now part of the Zorba menu. He was still close to my parents, calling them at least once a week for long conversations. They weren't the rope that had needed cutting.

El Centro downtown, which we bussed to that afternoon, was hot – too hot – and it was hard for the girls to understand what we were doing walking the busy market streets – hard to understand this was the destination, not just a long walk to get somewhere else. There were people selling everything, from cellphone cords to single Fruit Burst lollies.

Lena dragged heavier and heavier from my hand.

'When will we get there?' she asked, my own hand damp in hers.

'This is there,' I said. 'This *is* what we're doing.'

This only made her sag more heavily, until I was almost dragging her along.

It did feel hard to explain, even to myself, what this was all about, these seemingly aimless movements in which you leave your own life behind to wander around and, well, look at other people. Having my brother as guide made our movements both more logical, in that we were in some way seeking to visit his life, and less logical, in that we had no external reason to be here but him.

At Botero Plaza, outside the Museum of Antioquia, we looked at the Botero sculptures. Fernando Botero was born in Medellín and still lives here, just outside the city. A print of his exaggerated version of the Mona Lisa had been hanging at the girls' level in our kitchen since they were three, a present from their uncle Tom. Every Botero form in the square was an exaggeration of curves and lines, like swollen figures from *Gulliver's Travels*, except they seemed filled with a quite unSwiftian joy. As though they too might like to dance.

Inside the gallery, Botero's painting of the death of Pablo Escobar in 1993 gave a sense of the drug lord's scale here, as he lay across rooftops, a hugely inflated and now fallen figure above Medellín. At its peak in the 1980s, his Medellín Cartel is thought to have supplied 80 per cent of the global cocaine market. The city is now deep, we'd read, in its transformation from 'murder capital of the world' – once supposedly the world's most dangerous city – to city of 'urban regeneration'. The new tagline was being worked hard.

But it wasn't the painting I remembered most from my last visit; it was my brother standing in this gallery telling me how one of their roofers had been shot. I've spent ten years explaining to people in New Zealand where Medellín is, and why they think they might have heard of it. The follow-up questions about why my brother lived in the city were harder to answer. It was unquestionably beautiful, this city in the hills, and I could see the life my brother had built for himself was a good one, but I was still stretching to understand. Back outside in the heat, we got a family photo of the five of us in front of a giant horse.

By the time we got in a cab, Lena and Natasha were distinctly pink and floppy. With Tom in the front and the four of us piled on top of one another in the back, the girls immediately fell asleep, their small sweaty bodies a tangle of limbs with our own. It was hard to imagine ahead to a time when they wouldn't feel like a part of our bodies, let alone be capable of going to live halfway around the world – or have children of their own.

Back at the apartment we asked about the pool, but it was still closed.

Tom came around again that night for a meal of pasta with roast tomatoes and we ate on the balcony, the girls sure of themselves again in the apartment, telling us how they planned to wrestle crocodiles and caiman in the Amazon. While Tim read to the kids and got them to bed, Tom and I stayed outside talking.

'So, are you going out partying after this?' I asked, aware of the tug of my barely suppressed jet lag and parental exhaustion.

'God, sis, I'm thirty-six.'

His response was quick, almost gruff.

He was. This wasn't just a partying or traveller's interlude: this was his life. I was just beginning to see how the family image of him, the late, last, loved baby of the family, had ossified in some way since he'd been gone, failed to grow up alongside him. And also, how hard it was to dislodge. This was perhaps especially the case because he – and the stories we told about him – functioned as an expressive container for all our fantasies about a certain kind of existence.

Our talk drifted.

He told me about his motorbike trips around Colombia with various friends. He talked about how the arrival of Venezuelan refugees was putting pressure on Medellín, and how he and J. were working to get visas for a group of them to work at Zorba. Then he told me about an old Colombian girlfriend he unsuccessfully got together with again recently, and an amazing American girl who was passing through and who he only kissed.

'It was good for my confidence,' he said.

'How could you not have confidence?' I broke in. Again, this didn't fit the family story.

He shrugged my question off with a laugh. I noticed again the thinness of his shoulders.

The way in which women loved him – or he them? – had always been a big part of the family mythology, and also perhaps part of his problem, if it was a problem. We'd had an argument once when he was home visiting after he made a comment about the people in the Kilbirnie Pak'n'Save being 'dowdy'. There I was beside him, his feminist sister, most likely wearing jeans and a windbreaker, adjusting to pushing an ungainly double buggy. But that was already a long time ago now. Another time – again, a long time ago – he'd given me a thinking point, soon after Tim and I got together, about what do you do if an amazing new person walks past you in the post office line, and you just have to talk to them. How did you contain that kind of need? I had shrugged off that one, looking then for a home more than for new adventures – or an adventure within a home.

My brother's openness could sometimes feel like a demand to see the world as he saw it. It made him vulnerable, but people loved it. Loved him. People told him everything. He gave whomever he was talking with his complete attention, his eyes fixed on theirs.

As he was with me, now, out there on the balcony in the warm evening.

I reminded him how I used to read to him, the six years between our ages making me for a time an almost-adult to him as child. There was one Great Barrier camping summer when we read a David Hill novel aloud to each other to help with his reading.

He asked me, now, about my writing and teaching, and what I was excited about at the moment. I found myself stumbling about in the open space of my life, out of practice in explaining what I liked and what I wanted. We didn't talk about my new-now-old family, who were perhaps sometimes too present between us here anyway.

Each day's itinerary ended up being cut in half, our pace pulling towards compromise between the children's speed and desires and my brother's ambitious plans for us. At times, Tim was forced into the role of children's advocate, while I kept pushing on, prepared to hand us over.

'They like it where we are,' he insisted at one point, persuading us to stay on at the botanic gardens, aquarium and science museum in what turned out to be one of our happiest afternoons in the city. 'They need longer in one place,' Tim said.

One day, we went in a van on a tour to a small coffee plantation, part of a collective of family farms. The tour took us from planting coffee trees (Lena and Natasha invited to plant twin seedlings in a single planting hole), to harvesting beans, to roasting and brewing coffee. We shared lunch with our host, who grew up on this farm and who, despite being two hours' drive from Medellín, had been into the city only three times in his life. When we asked about this, whether he wanted to, he responded with, 'Why would I need to?'

On our drive back, my brother's friend who had come along told us how he'd lived illegally in New York for a decade, sent away from

Medellín as a young teenager by his father. He had needed to leave to be kept safe, he said.

Another day we swung up the hill in the neighbourhood of Santo Domingo in one of the glass cable cars for which Medellín is famous, part of the effort towards urban development in the 2000s, in this case bringing affordable public transport up the steep hillsides of the poorest barrios. Tom told us these isolated neighbourhoods were badly affected by the violence of the 1980s and 1990s.

People here dressed up. Despite the steep close quarters we swung above, roofs formed from rusty pieces of corrugated iron held down by bricks, there was little evidence of poverty in the neat clothes of those who got in and out of the gondola car. We all nodded politely to one another. Most of the women who worked in the kitchen at Zorba came from neighbourhoods like this and supported extended families.

Halfway up, the spectacular España Library by Giancarlo Mazzanti, built in 2007 in the centre of the barrio, was being repaired so we didn't get off. I saw the library last time I was here. With its massive irregular structure of black concrete built into the cliff, it was designed to merge into the city's geography. I remembered the inside of the library being awash with pools of natural light, and the way in which that light came in through many small windows. The construction was developed to allow those who entered to feel removed for a moment from the world outside.

Every morning I walked to the supermarket up the highway from The Ocean and came back with fruit we'd never seen before. And at the end of most days we went to Zorba, Tom insisting we join the queues which formed almost immediately at five o'clock every evening when it opened. Once we made it inside, we ate pizzas and piled-up green salads, drank cocktails and outlandish juices, and played endless games of cards. Lena and Natasha had never been up so late so regularly. We were a different family here, hanging out in restaurants, staying out, listening to live music, letting go.

But there were no curtains on the windows in our apartment, and the girls woke at dawn. We all got more tired each day. As we ate breakfast on the balcony, we speculated about the pool, imagining the pleasure of our immersion in it, cool and chlorinated. After four nights, when we packed up and moved downtown, the pool was still closed.

Our new apartment was on a busy city street, a thoroughfare from city to train station. Tom wanted us to have some time in a 'proper neighbourhood' nearer where he lived. While we appreciated this, the kids' second-floor barred bedroom window opened directly onto the neighbour's door and window, both kept open in the heat. We were staying next to a party house.

The day bled into night, and night into day.

We all woke at dawn feeling groggy.

Across the road a woman was setting out small pottles of some milk product. It was clear that once the sun was up, she and whatever it was she was selling would be in its direct blaze. An old man slept on the bare ground.

When it came to breakfast, I realised something was decidedly off.

Mid-morning, swaying on a train, I wondered what would happen if I had to vomit, or worse. I swung from a handle with closed eyes, hardly even looking out for the girls. A teenage boy offered me a seat; I must have looked pretty bad. Tim offered to take the girls on without me, manoeuvring close enough to my seat to pick up the conversation we'd begun before leaving the apartment.

'You can still go back,' he said. 'I can take them. We'll find Tom.'

But I shook my head. I couldn't let my brother down.

Tim and I had had questions about the excursion from the outset anyway, so perhaps it was also that I felt I should be there with the rest of them for this one.

'I'm fine,' I said.

Tim looked doubtful but didn't insist, turning back to Natasha and Lena, who were trying to tell him something. Taking advantage of the seat I'd been offered, Lena climbed onto my lap.

We were heading to Comuna 13, one of the poorest and supposedly once the most dangerous of the sixteen districts that make up the city. Tom had wanted us to visit the place and we'd convinced ourselves it would be okay. I think we thought to *not* go would be to imply we believed the stories of dangerous drugged-up Medellín, or, alternatively, that we failed to understand we weren't the people in danger here. Perhaps that was part of why it seemed better not to register our anxiety. At least Tom had arranged a guide from the neighbourhood, so money we spent would go back into the barrio. That had made the sense of voyeurism associated with the trip somewhat easier to ignore.

But it was the hottest it had been since we arrived in Medellín, and my stomach was bubbling as we got off the train. Tom met us at the station with Laura, who had lived here her whole life. Feeling uncomfortably bloated, I quietly undid the buttons on my skirt beneath my shirt.

I wondered what we looked like to her, a foreign family dropping in – it may not have mattered much from where – and paying to see her home.

She'd learnt English as an adult, Laura told us, precisely so she could do this work and earn a living as a guide. Her teacher, an older American man who ran a free English language school in the neighbourhood, would join us for lunch. As we walked through the crowded streets, Laura talked fast while Tim and I tried to simplify and explain to the girls.

In 2011 a series of outdoor escalators had been constructed, zig-zagging up the hillside under narrow ceilings of glass. As with the gondolas, the aim of the development was to cut through the isolation of the steep mountainside barrio, opening it up for residents to come and go, to visit and shop for food, get to and from work. Like the gondola, the escalator had become a tourist site. That was where we were heading.

As the streets sloped upwards, the narrow footpaths sometimes turning into sets of stairs, Laura pointed out the now famous murals and graffiti, striking depictions of local heroes. We paused beside a painting of identical twin boys. They had their arms around each other and birds on their shoulders, while behind them the city blossomed on the concrete wall.

'How old are you two?' Laura asked our girls as we stood beside the painting, making an effort to break through their shyness.

Lena answered softly, 'We're nine,' speaking for both of them as she sometimes does, Natasha happy to let her.

'About the same as these boys,' Laura replied. Then, turning to Tim and me she added, 'A good age.' She wasn't sure if there was a story behind this mural; they were just kids from here.

I agreed about the age. It seemed to come with curiosity and the beginning of an independent take, but with our girls, at least, a feeling they were still happy to stay close.

'Being here with them makes us notice different things,' I said.

She nodded and I asked if she had children.

'Yes, but older.'

I wondered how old she was – she seemed about my age, early forties, with long hair and tight jeans. When we bought lunch later, she got an extra meal to take home to one of her sons.

It was hotter in the narrow alleys, with small two-room houses close on either side. My palm was slippery with sweat in Natasha's hand, a headache coming on now too.

Then, just as the escalator came into view up ahead, we were met by half a dozen military police with semi-automatic rifles. Laura signalled us hurriedly off to the side of the narrow road. She told us the heavily guarded man approaching was the Medellín city mayor. We were too stunned by the guns to quite take it in. But we were a photo opportunity, a tourist family here enjoying a tour, and the mayor, who looked to be the same generation as Laura, greeted us and shook our hands while cameras clicked. I'm not sure, but I think Laura stepped quietly out of frame.

We moved on and stepped onto the escalator, where at least we could stop climbing stairs. We stood in the blazing sun and let the moving staircase take us up through the neighbourhood, people's homes close on either side, plants behind barred glassless windows, every building a basic rectangle with a flat cast-iron roof. Children sat out on doorsteps. Dogs lay in the sun. Once or twice, Laura exchanged greetings with people.

Her house, it turned out, was right at the top, a four-room structure in which she told us she'd grown up with her fifteen brothers and sisters.

'Fifteen?' I asked, repeating to the girls what she'd said, wanting to make sure my daughters registered this glimpse of another possible life.

'You know,' Laura said, to me this time, 'a man's strength here is shown by how many children he has.'

Her tone was dry. We were both thinking, I imagined, about a woman's strength.

Laura told us she now lived in the house with three of her brothers, along with their families and her own two children. They had a room per family.

You could see right down over the neighbourhood from here. The house's position at the top of the mountainside escalator made this a newly valuable view, the bowl of the city stunning in its cupped beauty. The barrio spilled down the hill beneath like terraced gardens, small homes with wonderful views if few comforts. One of Laura's brothers, who was building a new storey on top of their place, invited us to climb a ladder to the roof. Once we were up, Lena and Natasha held Tim's and my hands tight, staying well away from the edge.

By now, three hours into the tour, Laura was clearly tiring, repeating some of the stories she'd already told. But this was also the climax of the tour – her home. She was right here in 2002, she said, during Operation Orion, when the neighbourhood was under siege.

'I was here. In this house,' she said. She gestured up at the sky, at where armed military helicopters flew in and fired on the civilian neighbourhood. She and her family hid for three days.

Not wanting to interrupt her with questions, I was more than ever conscious of my lack of historical knowledge of this country with its long-running civil war, and so of the layer upon layer of complexity she navigated as though we too would know. It was a government military operation, she said, to regain control from guerrilla groups, including FARC. But they installed other paramilitary groups instead, right-wing ones this time.

'Over there,' she continued, gesturing towards a steep hillside across the valley. 'That's where they buried the people who were killed in those years. Hundreds. Thousands maybe.'

This was no longer a tour – it was testimony.

I had stopped trying to explain to the kids. They were beyond questions from heat and hunger anyway, which felt both urgent and unmanageably trivial as Laura talked.

'The bodies were cut up before they were buried,' she said.

There was an emptied-out weariness in her voice now, perhaps from the gap between what she was saying and what she really thought us capable of receiving. Or perhaps just from the repeated memory.

My brother stood awkwardly between her and us, wanting to

make it possible, this encounter, if that was what it was. He wanted us to know. He also wanted her to be okay, and in some way, to be heard.

I sat down on the rooftop, taking Natasha onto my lap this time, aware of the vast gap between our experience of life and this. How could we begin to understand this world? My children knew even less than me. I was aware, too, of the uneasy tension between Laura's seeming desire to tell and the financial imperative to exhibit her trauma to us via this tour. Now that we'd come, it felt like the best we could make of it, for now at least, was to pay and to try to listen.

I was also feeling queasier every minute, my concern about my own sickness and care for my children somehow obscene in the face of this other woman's experience. For her, obviously, this wasn't something children should – or could – be shielded from. And we'd chosen to come and to bring them.

I had been aware on some level from the beginning – and Tim more so – that this would be a form of dark tourism, even slum tourism, which we knew had a long, exploitative history. But if my brother lived in this city, and he and I were family, our places also must be related to this one. It might have been part of what he wanted us to see – why he needed to live relatively close to lives like Laura's, to acknowledge they were equally real. He'd been here before the escalator was built.

Laura dropped into Spanish, then, talking with my brother and her own.

After a bit, she switched back into English and, addressing Tim and me again, she said, 'It still goes on.' They had been talking about a friend of her son's in the neighbourhood who had recently been shot. 'It makes me anxious.'

She shook herself, glancing at our girls.

'But let's have lunch,' she said.

*

I almost couldn't go out again, but that night there was dinner planned at a Peruvian restaurant with a group of Tom's friends. I wondered for a moment if Laura would join us, before quickly realising this was a different set. They were mainly male expats, although some of the girlfriends were Colombian. One, Christina, gave our girls all her attention, allowing us to talk to other people until I wondered what her relationship with Kiwi Dan would bring her, he of the potential peanut-butter empire. Everyone here, it seemed, came and went from the city. One man ran a finca, a rural backpackers' of a sort, in the hills above Medellín, and had come down for the evening on his motorbike. His breath was sweet with pot when we kissed cheeks, everyone greeting me as my brother's sister, and therefore almost extended family to them too. There was the photographer fresh back from UN work at Chernobyl, and the couple on leave from a closer UN mission, helping with the collection of weapons from FARC fighters as part of the recently brokered, still fragile, national ceasefire. The couple had been living in a UN tent between a government military battalion and a FARC camp. The man in this couple too was a New Zealander, and they planned to move to Wellington the following year. I wondered how New Zealand would look to him on his return, and to his Colombian partner – what she would miss, what would seem strange, whether they would stay. There was also a guy who'd invented some gambling app that meant he didn't need to work. Tom wasn't so sure about him.

My best discovery was that Kiwi Dan knew Tom in Christchurch in the late 1990s. They were arrested together as nineteen-year-olds for being drunk and disorderly and kicking over a rubbish bin. They met again here in a queue at the post office (that place again), neither of them quite believing until they spotted each other a second time that the other had really ended up in Medellín too. I thought about what it was in those angry young men that had led them to move so very far away from home. Or, what it was in small town New Zealand – where my brother, at least, had never quite fitted – that had made them leave. Tom's South American fascination began with salsa dancing, which he did twice a week in a small upstairs bar just off Cuba Street in Wellington, one of the few men there, already miles and miles from Masterton where my parents then lived. Even at our tiny rural primary school of fifteen students, he was the one in flamboyant long shorts, with hair gelled up into a spike. Admittedly, it was the eighties. By the time he got to secondary school he was the punk skater kid at the private school, getting bullied because he wouldn't step aside – quite literally once, getting hit when he refused to get off a school path because a group of older rugby boys had told him to. He'd developed an almost painfully fervent reaction to things he felt weren't right. But while his going might be good for him, it left a rift behind in our lives.

I remembered as well that when he first moved to Medellín, having taken Development Studies in his mid-twenties and done a student exchange to Buenos Aires, he'd been determined not to spend his time with other foreigners. When they first opened Zorba they'd paid the travel websites not to feature it. This stance was influenced by the fact that ten years ago so many of the foreigners in Medellín were either sex tourists or American military. The only direct act of violence he'd experienced was when he was punched in the face by a drunk American, breaking his nose. He spent hours trying to get help, stumbling through the streets with blood all over his face and no one responding to him, because they thought him just another drunk foreigner. When he did make it to a hospital waiting room, as he told the story, an old woman waiting near him said, 'Aah, muchacho . . . no tienes familia aquí?' *Aah, young man, don't you have any family here?*

Now his closest friendships were with other expats. Perhaps this was itself an expression of shared homesickness. What this group seemed to share most strongly was a sense of being people who were not fully at home anywhere. This community of friends were also a part of what my brother wanted us – perhaps mainly me – to see. I wondered again about Laura, and what she made of groups like this and what they were seeking in her city. After dinner we were all meant to go out dancing, leaving Lena and Natasha with a babysitter, but I just couldn't pull it off and Tim came back with me. This was as far as we could get right then. Tom and his friends set off into the city lights.

We woke at dawn again and all the girls could say was, 'Please, please, can we swim today.'

Our attempts to find a playground had been unsuccessful too.

My brother's own apartment didn't have a pool. This was deliberate on his part, I'd realised over the past few days. An opting out of a particular kind of luxury. I was beginning to understand that this was also a refusal to purchase middle-class respite – a resistance to insulating himself from the difficulty of the world. He didn't want to live like that; perhaps he just couldn't. His previous apartment had been right downtown in El Centro, which we'd walked through on our first day and where he said he got a buzz out of seeing the dynamics of so many other lives. But he couldn't manage to live there full-time, as the thick polluted air made him ill with asthma. Unlike others who lived there, he had a choice. The current apartment was a compromise.

He'd been listening to his nieces, though, and I was feeling better today so he'd found us somewhere to swim, the apartment building of friends, a Spanish and Brazilian couple. For a long time the woman had been my brother's flatmate. At dinner the night before, I'd noticed how close the two of them sat, their pleasure in leaning into each other. She joked as we said goodnight that he'd missed his chance.

At the apartment complex gate we gave our names to the concierge and were let in through the entrance designed for cars. It was like another city in there, a number of buildings around a leafy courtyard. We got changed in the friends' apartment, where the walls were covered in photographs of the woman, who was a yoga teacher, doing poses on the grass. The boyfriend was an environmental engineer. This was another life again.

First, we went to a playground the kids had spotted. This, it turned out, was where the playgrounds were – inside these gated communities. It was a place I might have previously been embarrassed to use, judging the privileged who lived there. But now I sensed the desire for comfort that might be associated with it. An apartment complex and an apartment pool signalled something *apart*, sectioned off from the pressing specifics of place. Inside, we were released from the work of travel, and so also from the experience of the city.

When we finally got to the blue glittering pool, the girls leapt straight in, gravitating towards the other child in the pool, a girl their age. I watched them jump and move in a way they hadn't for days. They became loud, as I'd hardly seen them since we left home, shouting and diving with this new friend, slipping sleekly through the water. They'd been missing other children.

Beside us in the complex there was a Colombian version of a baby shower going on. There were speeches and laughter and loud music to mark the familial celebration.

Tom lay back with his friends, the three of them lapsing into Spanish, the friends clearly teasing my brother about something that made him laugh too. I was glad to see him laugh.

When Tim and I got into the pool with the kids, it was a relief to feel the cool water surround and lift my body, asking nothing of me. The pool suspended us. I caught one of our daughters and held her tight, enjoying the familiar warmth of her body against my own, then released her and let both girls swim around us.

I held my breath and put my head under, luxuriating in the quiet of it, sounds arriving only in muted form, disembodied legs moving around with slow, exaggerated motions of distant dancers.

But eventually it was time to get out. The weight of gravity gathered around us again as we emerged into the air and left wet through the gates into the city streets, the roar of motorbikes and cars kicking back in, only slightly quieter because it was Sunday. People were out walking or gathering to talk beneath the many street trees planted to help the city breathe.

Later that night, as we packed up for our morning flight, one of the girls declared this our best day in Medellín. It was the one when we weren't really here, I thought at first as I moved around the small apartment gathering our things and compressing them into backpacks, our swimsuits already dry. But then that didn't quite seem to capture it. Perhaps this ordinary day was also the time we were most here, living a version of an ordinary, if privileged, life. Comparatively, perhaps it was the life that came closest to our home one.

I thought of the visionary generosity of the España Library, with its deliberately small windows creating a similarly removed place for people to be away from the outside world. But, unlike the pool, the library was public space, accessible to everyone.

In the following weeks, anyway, when I overheard the girls telling other people about being in Medellín, it was the outdoor escalator they talked about too, and the gondola with blue butterflies beneath, the botanic gardens, the horse-riding we did one day in the mountains above the city, and the woman who had fifteen brothers and sisters and who had been shot at from helicopters. And Zorba, which was like their uncle's living room, but also not, because there were different people there every night.

Besides, my brother wasn't done with us yet. Two days later he would have us swimming in the Amazon.

Amazon

We lay in hammocks in the heat of the afternoon. We had books but weren't really reading them. Natasha, her loose hair coiling into ringlets in the humidity, pushed my hammock so I swung out towards the lake. Lena lay in another hammock with Tim, the two of them chatting quietly. We were at a small nature reserve in the Peruvian Amazon jungle. I looked over at my brother snoozing, his hands clasped across his chest, his face open and relaxed. He'd done everything to bring us here.

Looking back, this feels like the moment from which things really began to tip over.

We'd flown from Medellín to Bogota, then on to Letitia, a port town of 33,000 on the Colombian bank of the Amazon River. In preparation for our visit, Tom had done scoping missions to various parts of Colombia, which had begun to open to tourism after five decades of civil war. We needed to avoid the border regions with Venezuela, where economic and political collapse had already sent more than one million refugees into Colombia. We knew that was an utterly different form of movement, one our small family group wasn't well-equipped to meet up close, although Tom had plans to head to the border regions on his own on his motorbike. Finally, we'd settled on coming to the Amazon, where Colombia, Peru and Brazil meet. Tom had come back from this scouting trip to call us excitedly on the phone. He'd found the place for an adventure, he said.

Letitia can only be reached by plane or boat, the Colombian territory making little sense on a map, a small thumb jutting down to stake a claim on the river. The deep green jungle had stretched out beneath as we flew in. Tom had called the 'airport hotel' that he'd booked us a 'hut', so we'd been expecting something basic; instead, fifteen minutes by shuttle from the airport we were given gumboots, directed to put on insect repellent, and taken to the most magnificent treehouse we'd ever seen, a beautiful wooden structure in the rainforest, 5 metres above ground. The hut was encased in mosquito-proof screen walls, equipped with a toilet, and open so we could lie in our bunks and look out into the treetops. Later, a guide came and walked us to and from dinner in the dark, picking a path through the trees and pointing out a white milk frog clinging to a branch, deadly yellow-and-black poison dart frogs, and tarantulas I never managed to see. Insects whirred around us, making the dark seem to press closer. Lena and Natasha loved it, pitching in with information from David Attenborough and the Medellín science museum as we went, until they got hungry and tired and started asking how far to dinner. In the communal eating area, where we joined two small groups of Spanish-speaking travellers, we ate a dinner of fish and rice and plantain, pretty much what we would eat for every meal in the Amazon.

The next day a motorboat brought us further up the river – as brown and wide as a sea – and left us on a jetty on the Peruvian bank. There we were met by Walter, an Indigenous Ticuna man who had agreed to be our official guide while we were there. He looked to be in his early forties and wore the green and beige of a park ranger over his blue striped shirt. Smiling, he told us the plan, and my brother translated his words, or at least some of them. Tom's Spanish is good, but he's not an interpreter. It wasn't until we were off the jetty and walking into the jungle that I understood this was to be a proper walk, two hours rather than five minutes from riverbank to accommodation. It was hot – not as unmanageably hot as we'd anticipated, but sticky even in the deep green shadows of the trees, and we had no water, sunblock or insect repellent. We'd sent – it turned out – everything separately on a boat up the tributary stream. I pressed down a sliver of panic. There wasn't much to be done but tick my younger brother off a bit, and then try to relax into things. It hardly felt appropriate to complain. Tom wasn't used to travelling like this, with kids – and, it turned out, neither were we. We certainly weren't yet used to travelling with him.

I saw the girls themselves were enthralled, sticking close to their uncle, asking him the occasional question he translated to Walter and then back again. Walter walked quietly in the lead, giving us room to look and listen, stopping just a few times to show us processions of leaf-cutting ants, strange growths of epiphytes and, astonishingly, a metre-long spiky green iguana slipping into the water, and squirrel monkeys swinging through the trees.

Walter was wearing shorts, accentuating my awareness of our excessively colonial-explorer-style bug-off shirts and pants, already sticky with sweat. I wondered if we seemed like intruders to him, or like just another group of slightly comical Westerners whose visit could support his family. Or, more hopefully, like people who wanted to see something of his extraordinary home. Potentially, I guess, we were all three.

When we reached the lodge itself, on a reserve by a small lake where we were to stay for the next few days, Walter made it clear that we shouldn't leave the wooden decks of the place without him. The paths through the jungle were hard to find, and there were insects and snakes, animals and plants it was best we didn't meet on our own.

Safely deposited, we explored the platforms that linked the bedroom we all shared to the open dining room, verandas, toilets and cold showers, and what functioned as docks for kayaks and canoes. The outer floats were made of wood from the cashapona, or walking palm tree. On our walk in, Walter had pointed at one of them standing in the wet of the jungle floor on triangular tipi systems of stilt roots, adapted to survive constant damp. Everywhere else around us now was dense, palm-punctuated jungle, right up to the lake and decks.

The furthest platforms, including the one where we swung gently in our hammocks, were floating, designed to rise when the rains came. We were here in the dry season and for now the verandas rested easy under a perfect blue sky. So far, not even the mosquitos had been bad, no worse than on your average New Zealand camping trip, although we were spraying on repellent at every opportunity and, apart from Tom, eating malaria pills for breakfast. He'd told us not to bother, but on this one thing we'd chosen not to follow his advice.

On everything else, Tim and I had left my brother in charge – along with Walter, with whom he'd been exchanging text messages in the months since they met here on Tom's scouting visit. We were pretty much helpless anyway, without Spanish or Portuguese. In the process of handing over control we seemed to have outsourced many of the responsibilities and anxieties of travel too, especially the need to make decisions. Tom had given us a laminated itinerary when we arrived, detailed down to where we would eat each meal, time set aside for 'chilling / kayaks' (what we were doing now), and boats booked to get us from place to place along the river. There was no mobile coverage in the rainforest. We were completely in his hands, even more so than in Medellín.

As we rocked gently in our hammocks, the jungle provided a low background hum of insects and frogs, broken by the occasional screech of the two scarlet macaws who had been hanging around since breakfast. Nearby, the reserve's tame squirrel monkey, Lulu, nibbled on a small sweet banana. A great egret perched elegantly on a branch sticking out of the shallows of the lake. There were murmurings from the dining room, where a Colombian tour group had arrived for lunch, almost the only other guests. A few guides, Walter among them, played cards at a table on the next platform over. It all felt perfectly arranged.

As we moved from one experience to the next without really knowing what was coming, things that might have been nerve-wracking or uncomfortable largely felt exhilarating. That morning we'd all been taken in a small boat to the end of the lake. Then we'd climbed an enormous tree and ziplined across the water. When Tom had proposed this on a phone call to Wellington, I'd been a bit unsure about the girls doing it, but he'd suggested we book them in and see.

Even then, it wasn't the zipline but the boat that proved an issue. Tim doesn't like small boats and he sat somewhat grimly in the centre of the canoe on the wooden floor. We'd both been keen when my brother talked about us going to the Amazon, but Tim, at least, had been imagining jungle more than river. He'd never quite consented to be in this situation. A former climber, he couldn't wait to be out of that boat and at the top of the tree. It probably didn't help that earlier in the day we'd seen the jaws of a full-grown caiman, cousin to the alligator, snapping up a dangled offering of fish on string. We knew there were piranha in there too.

So, it was in fact a relief when Walter pointed up ahead at the ceiba we were to climb, the tree reaching above the forest canopy, its top branches like a tulip bowl held up against the sky. Or like an inverted, rounded cashapona, set on its head. Skywalker, I thought.

We were met at the foot of the tree by three young Ticuna men who had walked there to join us. There wasn't really a pause where we could discuss and 'see' whether this was a good idea; the kids seemed up for it anyway. While the five of us were helped into safety harnesses, Tom translated basic instructions and we stared at the small wooden platform a full 37 metres above. The first guide went ahead, then we climbed up two at a time, pushing hands up then feet, then repeat, Tim first with Natasha, who whizzed up, then me with Lena, who took longer, taking time to register her fear. There seemed no space for me to consider my own potential fear – I was all reassuring mother in the experience, making sure my small pink-faced daughter felt okay. There was something almost pleasurably primal about responding in this way. For a while, the two of us hung together mid-tree sharing a safety rope, our legs curled up to rest. If we didn't look down, it was a lovely feeling as we swung gently from the tree, hearts pumping.

Tom came last with the second guide, so it seemed a long time before we were all transferred to ropes on the small sky platform. From there, we raised the courage to look out across the unending forest canopy, so many versions of green, the lake stretching away into the distance like a river.

There was a lot of talking between the two guides then. Once Walter had left with the third man to cross the lake to receive us, they had switched to their own language. Then they explained to Tom in Spanish, who explained to us in English, that the girls weren't heavy enough to make the full distance across the water alone. Potentially, they would get stuck midway. They'd need to come across last, each strapped to one of the men. At home the girls refused to go into a dairy on their own to buy an ice cream, but they hardly seemed to baulk at this. They understood there wasn't actually another way. We tried to make sure they grasped what they needed to do. Once Tom was gone, we wouldn't be able to communicate verbally with the guides. The younger of the two blew the girls balloon animals out of plastic drink pouches while we prepared.

Then, one by one, Tim going first, we each took a breath and jumped into the air, riding a metal cable out across the wide-stretched width of the lake. When it was my turn, I gripped the handle so tight my hands hurt before I was able to force myself to leap, but then as the wire whistled above, and wind rushed by, a sense of sky and space blew outwards around me, in a fleeting feeling of airborne flight. Then from the small wooden platform on the other side, having left our children behind with strangers, we watched them too fly out, each screaming with what seemed to be a mixture of terror and delight. I laughed as I watched Natasha, who came last, hurtling across, unable to quite believe we were really doing all this, our boundaries here radically altered from what they were at home. It was Tom pushing us, I knew, even if he didn't quite know this himself, working from what had become his own version of normal. He wanted us to have these experiences, to give his nieces something they wouldn't forget.

The girls couldn't stop grinning as we abseiled down. Walter had brought the boat across the lake to meet us, and as we stepped aboard owl butterflies landed on our heads and arms. We had scaled the rooftop of the forest, then let go. I was glad to have been pushed.

It's only when thinking back that I'm forced to question whether everyone was equally happy about sacred, ancestral trees being roped up and climbed in this way. The fact that the activity seemed to be a version of Indigenous vine climbing transformed into adventure tourism didn't necessarily help. On the boat ride back, Walter told us one of the origin stories of the Amazon River is that it is a fallen ceiba, the trunk forming the main river, the branches its many tributaries. On the one hand, I still don't know if going up there was just a clumsy form of trespass. On the other hand, it felt like a homage to the trees and water, so different seen from above, and I am still filled with the sense of that.

The day before, almost as soon as we had arrived at the reserve, we had gone swimming. After sorting out our shared room, mosquito nets hung ready to be draped over each bed, we'd changed in the heat into swimsuits and headed to the pool. This pool proved to be part of the lake – it was a rectangle in the decking, invisibly fenced off underwater to keep out the piranha and caiman. Foliage festooned the pool's brown surface.

The girls were still keen.

Tom got in first, descending the ladder into the slick water, then standing awkwardly waist-deep as a small crowd of other guests from the lunchroom gathered. I couldn't understand the mixture of languages being spoken but there was much laughter. At first I thought Tom was the attraction, then two men from the reserve got into the pool too, holding between them a net they began to pull through the water, laughing again as Tom retreated into a smaller and smaller section of the pool. As the net came closer, Tom gave a high-pitched shout and jumped, at which the men in the pool and the others burst into still louder laughter, and then looked to be explaining something to him.

'Sis, sis,' my brother called, beckoning us over to his side of the pool, his dark chest hair plastered to his body. He was smiling but I sensed he was uncomfortable.

'They've got two baby manatee in here,' he said.

'What? Manatee?'

I remembered an image from one of the girls' books, *What Animals Eat*, of a heavy-looking water creature. It was something between a seal and a hippopotamus, but bigger than either.

'Manatee, Mama, we know about them.' Lena was pulling at my

hand. 'Remember? They eat water lettuce and hyacinth. Can we see them?'

At least they were herbivores.

The girls were jiggling about now and saying, 'Manatee, manatee, manatee.'

'In there?' I asked, still doubtful, nodding at the opaque water in which my brother stood waist-deep.

He jumped again. 'I just felt one.'

The net had Tom in a corner, the two local men reaching about under the water. Then one of them pulled a small dark creature out of the water into his arms. It wasn't much bigger than our girls. The man held the squirming shape against his chest, struggling to force it over to the ladder, where another man wielded an outsized bottle filled with some kind of milk.

I dredged up a vague memory that manatee were one of those water creatures that had evolved from land mammals – they were related to elephants, unlikely as that seemed.

Sea cow, that was their other name.

There was a tussle, then the men succeeded in forcing the pink teat into the creature's mouth.

After a long moment of refusal that seemed as though it might last, she eventually began to suck. She made a slow, deliberate, rhythmic sound, and we all went quiet, pressing in to watch.

It was still hard to make out what she looked like. When the girls and Tim and I went closer still, I crouched down and found myself gazing at one large, dark, blinking eye.

Once this calf was fed and released, the men began to search for the other one, running their splayed fingers through the water, and Natasha pulled me away.

'I feel sorry for the baby manatee, Mum.'

'They're just feeding them,' I said.

'I know,' she replied, suddenly seeming older than her nine

years, standing there in her red-spotted swimsuit. How I loved her sturdy legs. 'It just makes me sad,' she said.

I paused before responding this time, looking out across the lake water, where there might be room for wild manatee to swim. Then I admitted, 'Okay. Me too.'

How quickly wonder could be dispelled. I'd let my confusion rest me at sentimentality, but Natasha had quickly passed through to something else.

'Maybe they're twins,' she said, after a bit.

As we watched the second manatee calf being caught and fed, I was reminded of all those calves, lambs, and kid goats my brothers and I bottle-fed as children. These were the kinds of farming stories I nurtured my urban kids on – how we fed whatever baby animal we had that year, going out barefoot on dewy mornings and calling until they came leaping across the soaking grass.

'What do you think happened to their mother?' Natasha asked.

Right. That. I had no idea.

I remembered lying in bed at night at weaning time, listening to hundreds of older lambs bleating in one paddock, their many mothers calling from another paddock, crying to each other so loudly that inside the house my parents and brothers and I could hardly sleep. I'd thought about that weaning process after the girls were born, as I fed my own young quietly through the night. Of course my family's belated, 1970s-influenced return to the land, to spend days walking the hills and working with animals, had involved the cruelties of separation. I had no innocence here.

We watched the large soft mouth of the second manatee sucking from a rubber teat.

'It's a nature reserve, so maybe they rescued them?' I tried.

It was possibly even true. It was certainly easiest to believe that, but I'm not sure Natasha was convinced.

Later, at the next place, a guide we met from the Colombian side of the river was noticeably upset when he heard that manatee were being kept in a pool. To be exhibited to tourists like us. His reaction made clear these animals were likely as much a part of a human financial system as farm animals raised for meat. We would learn that the Amazonian manatee population, if not quite endangered, was definitely vulnerable, threatened by hunting and habitat loss. Tom noted that Walter avoided talking about them, or about any of the other wild animals on display, including Lulu, the squirrel monkey with huge eyes who, it turned out, should really have been nocturnal. Walter seemed to only come and go from the place as a guide; he lived his own life elsewhere.

But even before I understood about the manatee, as I stood there with Natasha, a little removed from the group around the calf, I saw that this pool was an enclosure as much as a protected space – a pool for keeping in as much as keeping out. Us too, in a way, having set ourselves up to be carefully contained and fed experiences. (I think we'd imagined it as ecotourism, which it also was.) And tourists like pools, so we'd been given one. Much like apartment dwellers in cities are given pools, I guess, only this time, with manatee to boot.

There had to be costs to buying in to all this containment.

Once the feeding was done, both creatures released back into the small enclosure and the others moved on, our family was left standing on the boards in our swimsuits, Tom already in the water. Somehow, and this is perhaps the hardest part to explain, we carried on in our intention to swim, gingerly making our way down the ladder. The pool itself was hardly a pool, I let myself think, almost part of another watery world. A habitat in itself. As with so many things, it felt necessary to hold on to – even allow – a complex mixture of emotions. And to leave undecided whether we should have simply stayed at home or, in the moment once we were there, stepped away.

The earthy water was out of the girls' depth and once we were in they clung to me at first, one on each arm, so I felt like an aquatic bird, a human animal myself, forging a path through the water and plants while my children's feet fluttered beneath. When Tim got in, they splashed over to cling to him. As the five of us pushed about, displacing volumes around ourselves, we imagined the manatee swimming down there somewhere, wary of the pale foreign limbs moving through their world.

That was the day before. Now, as we swung in our hammocks, our attention gradually focused on the lunch group. They were down on the platform, now, and stepping one by one into a canoe. Already it looked unlikely.

'It's like a prank about how many tourists you can fit in a Mini,' I said to Tim, waving vaguely in the direction of the group.

There were sixteen, maybe twenty people in bright orange life jackets. They were being arranged two abreast by their guides, each teetering for a moment on the wooden seats as they stepped inside.

'Looks like they're all going into the one boat.'

We laughed.

Until we realised they were.

Then gently, as if in slow motion, their boat tilted. The woman stepping on in that moment panicked, wobbled, leaned, and the boat slowly tipped, cupped in water, and began to sink. Just like that. Men and women called out as the wooden floor floated slowly down beneath them.

We stopped our swinging and woke my brother. The people were toppling over one another to stay upright, reaching for the platform, seeming confused and dazed, not quite registering what was happening. Their movements were slow and ungainly, awkward versions of failed swimming, surreal in the rising water.

We finally came to properly, dropped our books and rushed to the platform to try to help. But the reserve guides' approach was leisurely and relaxed, then after a moment quicker but still a walk, and that seemed to set the tone. Nothing to panic about. Nothing unusual. No need for drama.

The boat was still holding people up, although they stood waist-deep in water now, throwing cameras and phones into the hands of those of us on dock. The only help I managed to give was to move a pile of electronics out of the way of sodden bodies still struggling to get ashore, hands held out.

I wondered how many of them were thinking of the caiman we'd all seen being fed a few hours ago. I was thinking of the caiman. Tim and the girls scanned the waters for its eyes and jaw.

'Wouldn't want old Snuggles around,' Tom said. The pet name hadn't seemed properly odd until that moment. And then, 'How many people did they *have* in that boat?'

'A lot,' we said.

Once everyone was ashore, a calm descended, likely rendered more serene to me by my lack of understanding of the quiet conversations going on all around us. Walter was there too, and he and Tom stepped aside together, exchanging what seemed to be chuckles of disapproval at the group's boatees, which I found only somewhat reassuring.

An hour later, there were bills and phones laid out on the decks to dry, and the canoe was still sunken, floating empty beneath the water. One woman wore her life jacket still, hunched on the deck, curled up in shock.

Tom crouched down beside her and gently said what we took to be, 'You all right?'

Afterwards he translated her response. She never wanted to get back into that boat, she'd said, and wanted to get out of the Amazon altogether. Right now.

The two desires weren't mutually compatible.

'Poor thing,' Tom said with pity as he told us, but also with perhaps a hint of that laughter. As though to say, what is this woman doing here?

I couldn't stop thinking about her.

It was in this moment – after we'd seen the boat sink, had taken our children by the hands, and happened to stand quietly beside the pool again – that we saw the manatee properly. We stood still, not speaking or moving, trying not to make our presence felt. The bodies of the two baby creatures rose in slow, graceful movements to pluck gently at foliage on the surface – two ghostly swimming animals moving within waters they claimed as their own.

That afternoon we walked for an hour in the heat through the jungle to Walter's community. The plan was to meet a motorboat at the village wharf that would bring us back along the main river. We moved quietly, following Walter's steps. Often it didn't look to us like a path.

From time to time Walter warned us not to touch particular plants or insects, but there was no longer danger of creatures such as jaguars, he said, which his father used to encounter here coming down to the river to drink. The large mammals that are left have retreated deep into the jungle, far away from people and the noise of boat traffic. Eventually, we came out of the shade of the trees into a clearing of crop gardens, empty in the heat of the day. Walter pointed out areas recently burnt to help their fertility. Small controlled fires still smouldered, and among the cassava plants and plantain trees heavy with fruit there was a smell of ash in the air.

The community itself was a bit further on, a string of small weatherboard houses on the bank of the river, on stilts for when the waters rose. This walk wasn't usually part of the 'tour', but Walter had invited us to come, possibly at Tom's request – I hadn't quite been able to tell. Either way, this was typical of my brother. He could meet someone at a crosswalk and they'd end up inviting him home to meet their mother.

Regardless, we all seemed large and white and out of place as we walked along the concrete footpath which formed a kind of main street – or the only street – through the community. Walter walked slightly apart from us, a few metres ahead, my brother a little behind him. Our daughters moved in close to Tim and me, looking at children with a litter of puppies outside one house, and further on at kids playing soccer on a court on the riverside. In many of the houses there seemed to be not much at all, except perhaps hammocks roped up for the day. People slept on the covered verandas in the muggy warmth of the afternoon. Every now and then we glimpsed the flicker of a TV or a small white refrigerator. Walter had talked with a degree of ambivalence about the arrival of electricity, and the guide we had a few days later had to leave us to attend a vote on whether his community wanted electricity at all, many members wary of how it would change things. The guide wasn't sure which way the vote would go.

We walked in silence. We tried not to stare. Tom asked me not to take photographs. As if I would. My mouth felt stiffened shut; only once did I manage to exchange a smile and nod of some sort of recognition with a mother preparing food in the midst of three small children.

In a small open-air hall, two lines of young teenagers faced each other and began to dance. Tom dropped back to us, murmuring that they were dancing the bachata, more beautiful even than salsa, he said. He'd been trying to learn it.

Walter let us pause, but not for long; these school kids weren't dancing for us. As he moved us on, I hoped he was on some level glad, though, to have us glimpse the dance and the way it was part of his community's everyday.

When we reached the end of the houses, we went into the small single town store and, at an outside table, shared beers cold from a fridge. There wasn't much for sale in there, but there was hard liquor. Lena and Natasha whirled straws around in their Letitia Colas. I watched the slow progress of a young woman heading back from the riverbank with a toothbrush, her long hair wet, and a bottle of the same Pantene shampoo I used at home.

Then, finally, we followed a narrow path through the vibrant green waist-high grasses to the river itself, now at its lowest point about 100 metres from the houses.

Walter told us the river has been rising less in the past few years, so that sometimes it didn't reach the crop areas dependent on yearly flooding. Other years the waters rose higher than they'd ever known. Before we came, we'd been reading about the upcoming Brazilian elections, and about Jair Bolsonaro, then just the leading candidate, and how he planned to scrap protections on Indigenous land rights and limits on deforestation. No one here had passports, and Brazil was close enough to this Peruvian riverbank that people could come and go for lunch. Ticuna were spread across the region. Within months, Bolsonaro would be elected president and by 2019 huge sections of the Amazon would be burning, being cleared for yet more large-scale cattle farming and soybean ventures. One of Bolsonaro's policies was predicted to create twice the global carbon impact of the whole United States economy, and it was this, with its potential to damage the Amazon's function as global carbon sink – as the 'lungs of the planet' – that seemed to create most concern in the newspapers we read, certainly much more than the impact on Indigenous lands and already vulnerable local populations. As great a percentage of the Colombian Amazon was also being cleared, at an increasing rate since the 2016 peace accord. Prior to this, FARC guerrilla fighters' occupation of the jungle had produced an incidental protection.

My brother passed on Walter's comment that it is easier to live here at this time of year, but the wet season, when everything is flooded, is even more beautiful.

Then, looking ahead, I saw our motorboat.

It did have a motor, but that only made it sit deeper in the water. The motor was a converted scrub-cutter. The wharf was a slight, narrow plank raised on sticks above the sandy shore. The boat was a smaller, more rudimentary version of the canoe we'd seen sink just a few hours before, and this one was to be ridden on the open river. By us.

Things sped up. Tim and the girls, who had gone ahead a bit with Walter, were already moving on. Tim glanced back at me with a look I refused to read, as he gripped our daughters' hands. They and Walter were on the makeshift wharf and then in the boat. And then Tom and I were there too and I was stepping on, gesturing to the man and his skinny son at the back of the boat about life jackets, when clearly there weren't any. There was no other way back.

Tim was down on the floor saying nothing and then my brother was sitting on a plank seat beside Natasha, and I was hunched beside Lena, and we were pushing out into the Amazon River, as wide and terrifying as the ocean, except with currents and submerged sticks, and piranha we couldn't see but that we'd watched on YouTube stripping flesh from bone. I could say nothing to the man just behind me who directed our course, although we were almost close enough now for me to feel his breath, the slight shifting of his son on the back bench. I was calculating whether I thought my girls could swim the distance we were from shore and whether I could swim with them and whether I would see caiman if they were here in this rushing body of water. The other bank was so far away it was another country.

I felt a flood of anger mixed in with fear.

I hissed at Tom it had to *get communicated* to Walter at the front and the man at the motor that we had to stay near the shore.

'We can't go out too far,' I said loudly. 'You said there'd be life jackets.'

I may have been shouting. 'My girls, my niñas, can't swim. Not well enough.'

I glanced at Tim, then quickly away.

I was shaking my head and gesturing with my arms.

I scanned the water, half standing now, my arm still hooked around Lena. '*Tell* them,' I breathed to Tom.

He was in the middle, as always, calling things in Spanish to Walter who shouted them back down the body of the now quivering boat to the pilot.

Then Walter sent something sharply back, which my brother translated at me. 'The pilot says you have to stay still. Don't wobble.'

It was a jolt.

I'd seen what happens when you wobble.

I sat down, gripping the side of the boat and gripping Lena too tightly, so that she shrugged, pulling away from the weight of my arm. I tried not to move. I continued to mutter stuff but more quietly now. Tim and both our daughters were uncharacteristically silent. The boy behind us with his father hadn't said a word. We all sat very still.

The small boat moved down the river with our small family balanced precariously along its length, as though along my own curved spine. I had brought us all here, to this.

It was hard in that moment to remember why.

My initial shock reaction, a drenching of maternal fierceness, began to seep away into a feeling only of helplessness. I could do nothing but sit still, and hope – and try not to do anything that would cause other people to get hurt, including those in whose company we floated. We weren't the only people in this boat.

After what seemed a very long period of rigid silence, Tom turned and said, 'Relax, sis. I've told them. I just couldn't while you were yelling like that.'

He swivelled and said something more to the pilot I was glad I couldn't understand.

Then he turned back to me, smiling nervously. 'Chill, sis. You worry about them all too much.'

After that, we hunched uncomfortably on the boat without talking for a long time as the stillness of the evening settled around us. I'd taken off my watch in the damp, but Walter had told us the boat ride back would take about half an hour. Right then, that was forever.

Earlier in the afternoon there had been talk of spotting pink Amazonian dolphins, but now I only hoped we wouldn't see them and be tempted to go further out. I would rather not see. I'd rather leave the dolphins to swim as they wished. My fear rode with us, as within me it began slowly to slacken. The sky gradually became gentle pink and orange, the water smooth in reflection.

It was not irrational to be afraid, I have to tell myself even now, and in doing so I notice how very afraid I am of showing fear, and I wonder about that. If (*if*) I am responsible for the formation of my daughters' courage, I am also responsible for their safety.

At some point, my brother said more gently, 'I did ask for life jackets. Before we set out.'

It meant something to hear him say that. It was an acknowledgement.

And later, 'We'll be okay.'

Then we were quiet again, almost close enough to shore to imagine swimming. I am not a good swimmer – I could not hold us up, or stop my children being swept away. This was not somewhere we could swim.

I saw then how closely my brother was holding Natasha in the boat, his arm around her shoulders.

Between us all Tim was quiet, sitting on the bottom of our floating craft.

Then he said, 'Look. It's beautiful.' It was quiet, but insistent. It was a hand held out.

Tim was all right. I had felt responsible for that too, hardly daring to think about him. But he'd seen there wasn't much to be done and so had just gone with it. It might have seemed to be one of the conditions of being involved with my family. In the scale of things, it might have felt no more risky than anything else.

'Yes,' I returned, also in a whisper, and despite Tim's admitted nervousness, or perhaps because of it, he felt like an anchor there, sitting cross-legged in the centre of the boat, a solid link to our other life.

Finally I could believe we were not going to drown. Our daughters were not going to drown. Not this beautiful evening.

When we stepped off one by one at the dock, I tried to thank the pilot, our host, gesturing at his child and my own and trying to make some connection between them; he would not meet my eye. My brother and Walter's farewell to him was long and profuse. Glancing our way, the three men laughed.

It was getting dark now and there was another boat journey to be had. It was in the shallows this time, in a canoe travelling between mangroves down the small stream that slipped from the river proper to the lake. Here if we tipped in we could wade to shore. It seemed unlikely that a caiman would be just waiting there to catch us.

Once we'd arranged ourselves onboard and pushed off, the loudest sound was Walter's paddle, dipping in and out of the inky water. He was a silhouette at the front of the boat. I realised he'd taken off the military green uniform jacket of the nature reserve staff before taking us near his home. I realised also that he hadn't pointed out his own house, which we must have walked right past down the single central path. At lunch he'd talked with Tom about how he wished he knew how to speak Ticuna. He'd stopped learning when he was young, after he was told he should only speak Spanish. He also spoke Portuguese. Ticuna is an isolate language, with around fifty thousand speakers, and apparently it was seeing a revival, with increasing bilingual education. I was glad to remember the easy linguistic switching of the younger men who helped us climb the ceiba tree, but I wondered where that left Walter.

My daughter leaned her head against my shoulder. Both of us were tired and still in the gathering darkness. There were fireflies, and again the deep-throated calls of frogs.

We started when Walter asked if we'd like him to bring a baby caiman into the boat. Before we could respond he put his paddle down and grabbed one, holding his hand tight around its neck so it couldn't bite. He invited us to touch its snakelike skin while its soft neck, vulnerable and exposed, pulsed fearfully between his fingers.

As we turned off our torches and slipped on through the night, I considered how many times he must have had to do this to thrill visitors. My brother had told us about it from his exploratory visit, when it must have seemed spontaneous. In the torchlight Walter had been smiling, laughing gently as the creature squirmed, but he had also looked weary. The baby caiman seemed, then, like part of the performance we'd all been participating in, of high-wire ziplines and boat rides and caiman feedings, all carefully orchestrated to give the feeling of experiencing danger up close, while just a jolt away, out of sight, there was real danger, real loss.

I thought of the pilot's slender boy out on the river each day. Of the everydayness, for him, of riding a precarious wooden boat between villages. And of the now changing river. I thought of Walter not knowing his family's language. And I recoiled from my small, neo-colonial drama of panic for my children – at my naivety in believing life jackets would be provided to keep my children safe. I struggled with the immediacy of my feeling that, of all people, they must be protected. Like everyone else, I'd seen the footage of boats sinking in the Mediterranean carrying thousands of refugees, children among them.

Four days later we would wait on a small jetty for a last ferry to take us back down the river to Letitia, then we would fly in different directions – my brother back to his life in Medellín, and my family and I continuing our travels then returning to our lives in Aotearoa.

In the days in between we would visit a monkey sanctuary, where former hunters worked to rehabilitate primates rescued from captivity or hurt in the wild, and we would spend a night in a backpackers in Puerto Nariño, the pedestrian-only capital of the Ticuna tribe, a place of six thousand people on a small lovely inlet on the Colombian side of the river. We would stay in the 'Jungle Lodge' of Calanoa, sleeping in a two-storey wooden cabin with a woven palm roof and a view of the river, and be led on another night walk of tarantula and scorpion sightings. On the short unguided stretch back to our cabin after dinner, one of the girls' torches would light up a tarantula. Just sitting there, long hairy legs curled around the railing where she was about to put her hand.

On our last day, we would experience our first and only rainforest downpour. One moment the five of us were playing cards outside, and five minutes later rain was falling in waterfalls, the wind blowing chairs over and mosquitos rising from the ground. Our family group would be rushed into the kitchen and surrounded by large chatty women wanting to talk with us about twins. My brother would tell us that throughout the trip he had been having to explain to people that our daughters are not his daughters. I wondered if he would get the chance to have children, or if he wanted to. I would become fully aware of how much love had gone into this journey, and of the longing my brother must have felt, too, towards our lives.

By the time we waited on the jetty later that last afternoon, the rain would have lifted and in the stillness we would see a dolphin break the surface of the water. It was not one of the rare Amazonian pink dolphins we'd hoped to see, but a freshwater dolphin all the same, a creature we hardly knew existed until we imagined this trip – much like the manatee. Soon we saw more of them, half a dozen small pale shapes leaping and diving in and out of the moving currents of their river, oblivious to us. The sky was a deeper blue after the rain. We stood alert on the rocking platform this time, willing the dolphins not to leave, not just yet.

Another week later, we would take Natasha to the hairdresser to have a substantial portion of her hair cut off because the week of Amazonian humidity had turned her curls into an intractable and expanding knot. I kept wanting to stroke her shaven skin, lift the remaining hair and touch her newly exposed scalp.

But for the moment, we were still together on a small wooden canoe floating through the night. And beyond anything, I was thinking about my brother, now a man in his mid-thirties, full beard and moustache, as at ease in Spanish as in English, and of how hard it seemed to imagine him coming home. He was better than I was at inhabiting places far from where we'd grown up.

I was aware of my daughter's head still heavy against me. She was so quiet she could have been sleeping, pushed in so close as to almost form part of my body. I watched her twin sister, beside Tim but leaning out, holding her hand above the water as though she wanted to trail her fingers through its blue-black surface. I resisted the urge to say anything, to tell her to be careful.

I wanted to reach past my partner and children – past my new family – and touch my brother's shoulder, although I'm not sure if it was to lean out with him, or to bring him home.

Desert Swimming

Phoenix

The bus from the airport to the rental-car hangar left full every two minutes, and that was just from one terminal. The hangar looked like a stadium as we approached, a circle of bright lights, a whole city of parked cars ready to transport. The cheery woman at the counter tried to persuade us to upgrade to a larger vehicle. We had arrived in the land of the car. The air was dry.

At the restaurant in our airport hotel we perched at a high table and ordered tortillas. The muted TV screen was filled with Trump. It was mid-terms and he was in his element at a rally for a climate change denier. The name Kavanaugh cut by in closed captions too, Trump's large orange face looking serious and filled with sorrow for his Supreme Court nominee accused of sexual assault. There was mention of the 'caravan' of refugees approaching from Central America, an invading army. A joke was made and laughter was indicated in square brackets, echoed aloud by a group at one of the bar tables. The four of us ate in jet-lagged silence, watching the comfortable faces rage.

In the fold-out sofa bed in our room, identical more or less to rooms at the lower-priced end of the approximately 5284 other Hilton Hotels in the world, I couldn't sleep. My thoughts were busy with politics, with where we were, with the conference we'd come to attend in an almost equally generic if glitzier hotel downtown, taking another of the 62,000 hotel rooms available in Phoenix. In an effort to calm myself, I read. First I tried a *New Yorker* article on Google versus Uber, then an essay on general apocalypse by Chomsky in the latest *Best American Essays*, and then an article in the *Guardian* about climate change. Unsurprisingly, the reading didn't help with the sleeping.

And that was without reading about where we had arrived. So far, all I really knew was a rough outline. Phoenix has been a textbook case in urban sprawl since the 1970s, and is now the fifth most populous city in the United States, and the fastest-growing. It has been described as the least sustainable city in the world. Its average annual rainfall is less than 200 millimetres, and like many cities in the American Southwest much of its water comes from Lake Mead, over 450 kilometres away in Nevada. The reservoir is fed by the Colorado River, and due to long-term drought and systemic overuse – Lake Mead supplies water to around 25 million people – both river and lake are at crisis levels. Their waters are dwindling. Fast. In 2018, the region was in its nineteenth year of drought. The city has sophisticated systems for storing groundwater, but it is still a city in the desert.

Then it was morning and our daughters woke at 5:15am, despite the blackout curtains, and they were exuberant and mad with excitement about the buffet breakfast and the hotel pool. I crawled between them in the king-sized bed we'd given up to them, and they each told me about their books, one giving a scene-by-scene rendition of *The Railway Children*. When Tim woke, we rode the elevator down, staring with dazed, sleepy eyes at the remoteness of the Sonoran Desert seen through glass beyond a vast sprawl of highways and low-rise hotels. November is the beginning of cooler weather here, but already the day was heating up.

In the restaurant we gobbled down plate-loads of hash browns and scrambled eggs and fruit and toast and croissants and two kinds of juice, and then more hash browns, because what else is a buffet breakfast for? Heaving full, the girls and I headed outdoors to the pool.

We had all the time in the world.

Empty of other guests in the early morning, the pool was standard-issue blue, with rectangular lines cut into two adjoining diamond shapes. For glamour, I presume – the Expedia photos had looked spectacular. I thought only fleetingly about where the water came from before we were all in the balmy, clear, frictionless liquid, tossing beach balls and playing tag. This felt like precisely what the pool was for.

The sun had not yet made it down into the well in the centre of the hotel where the water lapped. When I started to get cold I shifted to the even more luxurious spa.

Tim arrived with coffee.

We talked about the hotel rooms surrounding us, rising floor upon floor towards another rectangle of clear blue. The other guests slept on, stacked on top of one another in their pillbox rooms.

It seemed impossible to care about much from in here, not climate change or Uber or inequality or refugees. In the water, in the spa, in the pool area, in the hotel, in the hotel complex, in the airport zone, in the city, in the desert.

Ah, the desert.

Still, it seemed impossible to worry much.

There are no water restrictions in Phoenix.

There was air conditioning to cope with the heat. I wouldn't think about how it also caused the heat.

The water where we swam was so pleasant.

Everything is already in motion. The land of the car and the hotel room, for those who can. Road, route and destination have been pre-programmed. We are all to be in self-driving cars.

People won't change, so the people say.

It was so very comfortable in the spa, limbs limp. My children were so happy swimming in the chlorinated blue water, above them their own piece of rented sky.

We could swim until checkout.

Arcosanti

We arrived at the collection of vaults and open-air asps in the early evening, blocks of concrete with circular windows jutting up from the desert, steps and paths mazing between a foundry, an amphitheatre, apartments, and a communal dining area all built into one another. There was a surprising feeling of rain in the air. The only people around were gathered on the curved roof of a 10-metre-high concrete vault, watching explosions of lightning against bruised clouds. It was another planet.

Leaving our car outside the perimeter and our luggage for later, we joined the cloud-watchers, climbing single file up a steep ladder, keeping well clear of the sheer drop. They turned out to be people in their early twenties, here for the five-week workshops that have been running on and off at this planned architectural community for nearly fifty years. We were welcomed into the quiet group, our daughters lying back between our legs, leaning their bodies into us as the air got colder, all of us looking at the size of the sky. No rain fell, the flashes of lightning becoming gradually more distant. Slowly, everything turned a luminous golden, washed in varnish, and then the place dropped swiftly into the star-studded velvet dark of desert night.

Tim had booked this place months before, getting us the 'Sky Suite', one of the few parts of the complex available to outsiders as accommodation. About sixty people call Arcosanti home, and there is a fluctuating number of people here at any one time for workshops in ceramics or in the bronze foundry, and to learn about and help with the ongoing construction of the place. There are sometimes young architects here on internships from local universities, or larger gatherings here for music festivals or performances in the outdoor Greek-style amphitheatre.

When we told friends about our trip – both before and after – Arcosanti was the main thing Tim talked about. A year on, he would come back with a photographer to make an artwork here.

But for now, our family was just glad to have arrived in the striking otherworldliness of this place in the desert. Built by voluntary participants beginning in 1970, Arcosanti was conceived of as an 'urban laboratory', an experiment in the 'radical reorganisation of the built environment'. This place was all about imagining how to live. After Phoenix, being here was a relief.

Our Sky Suite was basic but beautiful, on the highest point of the complex, with curtainless ceiling-to-floor windows open on two sides. It was the best accommodation in the place but it still cost less than anywhere else we stayed in America.

When we woke at dawn the first day, there was a rim of orange all around the vast bowl of desert in which it turned out we'd slept. The light deepened, spilling colour into the day. We cooked toast directly on the gas hob and the smell reminded me of camping trips as a kid, and of our first night in Medellín with my brother. Tim and the girls settled on the platform in front of the east window, their books and cups of mint tea forming a shadow, a sculptural silhouette, framed by a circle against the gradually developing blue. We were paused. It was like a study in small to vast, a study in the scale of the sublime. Family and world. Family in world.

*

Once it was fully morning, we went to the dining area. The room was formed from square blocks with two-storey-high circular windows, and in this second breakfast we were joined by forty or so others. Those we'd met the night before smiled acknowledgement before heading to other tables, their hair still tousled, their faces soft with sleep. It had something of the communal feel of a university residence dining hall, with the crucial difference that those on duty serving and clearing up were part of the same community as those eating. An older couple who looked like long-timers kept to themselves over coffee. We'd heard that some of the residents had been here from the beginning.

After everyone dispersed to various tasks, the four of us went outside and sat on flat rocks beneath olive trees to read and write. Since we'd taken the kids out of school, we were making them write trip books to compensate, an activity which they were by now often seriously resistant to. We'd resorted to timers: write for at least ten minutes a day, sometimes two sets, and I wrote with them. It didn't seem a long time to spend composing one's own experiences of the world. Lena's best entries took the form of comic strips depicting her and Natasha swinging from trees with exaggerated curly mops. They liked their drawing books more. Lena had drawn a minute map of each place we'd been, trying to see how it all connected, while Natasha sketched flowers with a blithe lack of interest in our suggestions we find out what the flowers were called. We'd found no flowers here, but before driving north we had seen desert wildflowers in the botanic gardens in Phoenix, including outlandishly gorgeous cactus blooms.

When they were done and getting restless, Tim tried to explain how the cliffs had formed, from basalt boiling up. Arcosanti is on a mesa, a tabletop in the desert, so we were above a valley where sets of smaller cliff faces stepped up in brown-red rock. Our bare feet were deep orange from the dust. On a path down the hill below us, four young women moved rocks by hand, working on improvements to an irrigation system. Tim pointed out the solar panels on all the buildings, angled to the sun. In Phoenix, despite over three hundred days of sunshine a year, the most of any place on the planet, only 2–5 per cent of its energy is solar.

We joined a small tour group of day visitors later in the morning and watched the workshop participants hand-making wind-bells in the foundry apse. This was, at least notionally, how the community supported itself, and had been right from the start – it was part of the vision of the Italian-born founder, architect and urban designer Paolo Soleri. While designing a large ceramics factory in Italy in 1950, Soleri learnt to make ceramic and bronze bells, and the silt cast architectural structures of Arcosanti came from that imagining, the concrete walls of the buildings poured and curved like great bells hoisted to stand in the desert. The original plan was for the place to become an ultra-dense community of five thousand people, all living and working together, self-sufficient in terms of food and energy, and self-supporting through the production and sale of bells. Fifty years on, they were still making bells and it was clearly still a work in progress. The educational workshops, along with 'the Arcosanti experience' they offer, have become what keeps the place going.

Everyone fell silent during the pouring of the bells. Two bearded hipsters with a board between them balanced a heavy bucket of molten bronze as hot and red as lava, then slowly they tilted it, tipping the boiling liquid into moulds. When it was done, there was a relieved cheer from the workshop participants. It felt like a spiritual practice of sorts – practical but moving and, in its handmade approach, from another time.

Our guide, a young woman in a clean white T-shirt and jeans, led us through the maze of concrete structures. I kept thinking of her as a typical American VSA-type, eager to explain things and 'do good'. I had to remind myself that this was America too. We were still in America.

Our children moved close to the other kids who had joined the tour with their family, and our guide showed us how the separate apartments interlocked with one another, a window seat (our window seat) someone else's ceiling. People lived separately, but light and heating were shared. One apartment was built into the wall of the foundry, so that from one set of windows it was possible to watch the working of the bronze, with no separation between workspaces and living areas. To apply to become a resident, you had to write a letter of intent to the Foundation board and say what you could contribute. Even then, it was a long time before you could hope to get a shared apartment on site, and usually you'd spend time in 'The Camp', a collection of basic houses and greenhouses a short walk away. Work could be exchanged for rent. Living here, I calculated as I listened, was relatively affordable, even if the workshops themselves looked pricey.

Arcosanti's founding text was in our apartment – Soleri's *Arcology: The City in the Image of Man*. Arcology = architecture + ecology. The idea was that the built environment should be at a human scale: compact, pedestrian, car-less, building upwards rather than outwards to maximise interaction between people and with the surrounding natural area. It was conceived in explicit opposition to the motorway-based urban sprawl of the 1960s and 1970s. Soleri was in Phoenix before this, our guide told us now, a protégé of Frank Lloyd Wright: he knew what he was talking about.

In our own twenty-first-century moment, rather than the slow reformation of 'our contemporary sustainability movement', one online source about Arcosanti informed us – and our young guide reiterated – arcology continued to signal the need for 'complete *reformulation* of how we exist within our environments'. Arcosanti itself was still imagined as a prototype, an ongoing experiment in how this might work.

When we entered a concrete tunnel between buildings, our guide stopped us for a moment.

'I think of this as an architectural lung,' she said.

It was not so much a passage as a space between vistas. We paused, breathing together in the momentary cool. The lung seemed to pulse with possibility around us.

When the tour was done the others returned to their cars to drive on, and we went down to the pool.

The sign at the entrance to the pool, *Please shower before swimming*, spoke of sweat and work and heat that rises well above 40 degrees Celsius in the summer months, although Arcosanti's elevation makes it generally cooler than Phoenix. Earlier that year, flights out of Phoenix had been grounded because extreme temperatures of 47 degrees Celsius made the air too thin for planes to take off safely. Who knew that was even a thing?

The pool glittered a perfect light blue. In this otherwise extraterrestrial place, it was uncanny in its familiarity. The water itself came from wells. I wondered why the pool blue paint persisted even here, but still, this pool felt different – embedded in a way that altered its relation to its surrounds. A basalt cliff face on one side was formed from rough rocks into which a stone room had been built, rounded windows open to the air. On the other side was a drop to a dried-up desert river valley. Like the apartments, the pool had been built into the rock and, all year round, took on the rock's constant temperature of 18 degrees. All of this was designed to make air conditioning unnecessary even in extreme heat.

The location seemed to make little difference to Lena and Natasha, who jumped straight in, but I thought perhaps it would make a difference in memory. Tim and I read and talked on the ground beside the pool, and I felt my thoughts slow and slip free. My computer and phone had been off for a whole twenty-four hours, which seemed right for the place, although in fact there was wireless everywhere. But the buoyancy of the water and the space of the desert made time open out. Tim was by then already beginning to talk about coming back. Only when Natasha floated past and we noticed her feet were a chilled shade of grey-blue did we get up, stretch in the warm air, and join them in the bracing water.

But then, in the afternoon, when we asked one of the residents in the community shop (which mainly sold bells, and was built high and bright on a floor above the dining room), how long he'd been here and how long he planned to stay, he laughed.

'To wait out the Trump years?'

It was a kind of question, said with his dark eyebrows raised, as though to say, how long will it take?

D. was in his mid-twenties; perhaps older, I thought when we were talking to him there in the shop, then younger later on when he was drunk and dancing in the dining room, doing crazy scissor legs while we ate slices of the generous square pizzas his friends on kitchen duty made for dinner that night.

He told us about the things that had brought him here – the fact no one listened to anything but discussions of free markets and economic growth during his degree, but also, more puzzlingly at first, about how the sports coach he'd named his college a cappella group after was fired for abuse of players.

I remembered the first time I heard an a cappella group singing. It was night and they were gathered beneath an arch on the Princeton campus, where I'd just arrived as a graduate student. The sweetness of their voices rose, unaccompanied, into the darkness.

D. paused in his wrapping of the small bronze dish we had chosen from the foundry. The girls had taken turns cupping its gold-green weight in two hands, deciding it should hold nothing but itself.

Then, in a rush, as our daughters wandered off to rock the smaller bells into tinkling music, D. started talking about Soleri. I wandered off too at first, but Tim called me back. 'You should hear this,' he said. D. had wanted to tell us why he'd sought sanctuary here, it became clear, because Soleri had now himself been accused of sexual abuse of his own daughter. It seemed, D. told us, his voice thick with emotion now, that many people in Soleri's inner circle had known about at least some of it. The Arcosanti board had been accused of cover-ups. The official apology half acknowledged as much, but not enough, D. thought. Although the abuse hadn't occurred here, he said that over the months since it had come out a number of younger residents had left the community. Soleri, who died in 2013 at the age of ninety-three, was, after all, buried here.

I felt little shock, just the familiar jerk of generalised anger in that year of Harvey Weinstein. I had a sick, sinking feeling as D. continued to talk. Even here. But, of course. What had we thought? This place was no pure oasis in the desert; it was filled with the world. That was part of what D. was telling us. Being here was not a straightforward choice, no more than anywhere else was. Evidently, it wasn't yet clear what D. himself would do, as he talked and talked in an effort to work it all out, our dish in his hands still not wrapped, our daughters, thankfully, involved in some game together in the bright stairwell. I noticed how often Tim glanced their way, making sure they were safe from hearing this. I felt the queasiness for him, as much as for myself. How to be a man in this moment? A good one? I touched his arm.

I later read the piece Daniela Soleri had written – her account of years of abuse, leading to her father's attempted rape of her as a seventeen-year-old. Part of what was striking about the piece was its articulate assessment of the dangers and costs of the idea of the all-powerful solitary genius figure, still too popular, and the behaviour such myths allow. She wrote that the problem with her father, despite his vision, was he was 'capable only of seeing others in terms of their role in his world'. It was this, she argued, that made the kind of abuse she had experienced possible. In Soleri's case, it had also relegated him to the role of isolated 'prophet in the desert', an individual ego limiting the radical potential of the collective thinking at the core of Arcosanti.

As we stood there in the bell shop, D. told us too about retrospective discussions some members of the community were now having about Soleri's wife, Colly Soleri, and how she had to an extent been sidelined from the project and accounts of its legacy. The integration of food into the urban environment had always been part of the vision, and it was Colly who was interested in agriculture, D. said. Paolo was more into the building than the growing. There hadn't been food grown at Arcosanti for a while, though the now small, murky pond in the valley below once formed part of an extensive irrigation system for gardens and there were now plans to revive it. Colly was supposed to have said, 'There's only room for one genius in the family.' As a quotation, it was possibly too good to be fully true, but it encapsulated the wider problem. D. was fully cognisant of the terrible neatness of the story he had to tell, adding as a sort of trump card that Daniela, who had resigned from the board and so was no longer actively contributing to future imaginings of Arcosanti, was a professor specialising in agriculture and food systems. Contrary to the vision of self-sufficiency and car-free lifestyles, those at Arcosanti now, like the rest of us, drove to the supermarket for groceries.

Tim and I kept talking about this in the days and months that followed, and about what Arcosanti was – simply a bizarre, aesthetically spectacular but ultimately barren relic of the 1970s, or a foundation block, or even a seed that might be re-germinated and cultivated in its good parts for a more viable future. Just as the

Me Too movement made it possible for Daniela to come forward in this moment, perhaps the urgency for new modes of living at this same historical juncture could make it time for visions like Arcosanti again, if hopefully not for men like Soleri. Or was the hubris of such foundation in the desert, indeed a city built in the *image of man*, too much to overcome? The failure of imagination, it seemed, might in fact lie in its *limitation* to 'human scale', in which humanity could only ever be conceived of as the subject, the victorious cowboy protagonist who must inevitably overcome everything in its path, even the desert. The egotistical fantasy of the technological fix.

I wanted to believe, though, that a place like this could continue to exist as an oasis, a lung, albeit one with the rattle of infection.

I wanted to believe, to hope, that the next generation could take a much-needed breath from the old and make something of it. We will need to reach back beyond our past two decades, and back beyond the neoliberal 1980s and 1990s, to some of the most radical thinking that came before – economic, social, architectural.

We have to be able to trust that it is possible to live together and to sustain one another, including men and women, fathers and their daughters.

But the place itself, and what it stood for, was no less altered by knowledge.

On our final night at Arcosanti there was a full moon. While our girls slept inside with damp hair from another swim, Tim and I sat out on the rooftop and – in the space of a breath – saw a shooting star. In the same moment, somewhere not far off amont the concrete curves, we heard the sound of young voices pealing out in joy, like wind-bells. And the pool where we had swum became a bronze dish, holding up its small burnished treasure of water against the drought-stricken sky.

Canyon Country

'The sunrise. Wake up.' Pulling me urgently from sleep, Natasha climbed on top of me in the bed we shared. Her knees hooked around me like a bony monkey. 'Wake up,' she said, louder now to wake Lena and Tim too, still heavy with sleep. 'Hurry or we'll miss it.'

We pulled ourselves from sleep and scuffled around in the cabin finding warm clothes and hats – it was chilly up here – then went out into the quiet, not light yet but no longer dark. We put our torches away, the girls hushed by the stillness. Ponderosa pines formed silhouettes around us as we picked our way through the dawn towards the canyon. The trees were spread out and the ground so bare we hardly needed the path.

Then, up ahead, an elk, a huge shadowy shape just standing there in the morning air.

We stopped, gathering in close.

Slowly he turned to look at us, the muscles in his neck seeming to work to hold up the weight of his antlers. Simultaneously heavy and delicate. Lines from Elizabeth Bishop's poem 'The Moose' ran through my head. Only, there it was a she – an otherworldly animal who, like this moose, slowly looks her viewers over. 'Why,' Bishop asks, 'why do we feel / (we all feel) this sweet / sensation of joy?'

There was a dim smell of elk, like farm animals but with more forest. Then, as if he had all the time in the world and was no longer interested in us, the elk turned his head away. He continued to stand there, his warm breath misting in the growing light. We were dismissed.

'Elks weigh from 325 to 1000 ibises,' Lena whispered.

The girls had been learning the weights of animals from the information guide, and pounds (lbs) had become *ibises* in their lexicon.

The elk became a flock of birds, a whole ecology of warm-blooded life lifting off.

We had arrived the day before. As we'd driven here, I'd imagined we would arrive at the bottom of the canyon as you do at Yosemite in California. I've never been a very well-researched traveller, and Tim had booked this one.

Instead, the ground dropped away.

We'd found out that it would be an overnight hike to get to the bottom of the canyon, going down narrow switchback paths cut through sedimentary layers of rock, and we weren't up for that. Instead, on the first afternoon we'd skirted parts of the southern rim, walking the Trail of Time, in which each horizontal metre of the walk represents one million years of vertical geological history, starting two billion years ago. We passed stones marking the time when all this was a shallow tropical sea, through to those marking the relatively recent period in which the now dwindling Colorado River cut the canyon itself, just six million years ago. We'd wandered along eating chips, our kids jumping on 200-million-year-old rocks and reading information panels aloud while teenagers teetered nearby, taking selfies and ignoring their parents' cautions.

It wasn't until after our dawn encounter that it felt real. In the morning air after the elk, so assured of its place in the half light, we walked on to the canyon's rim. At first, the layered rock was only visible in shadow form. As the sun rose, slanting light arrived and descended slowly into the canyon, moving down and back a period of geological time every few minutes.

The four of us sat on a narrow bench to watch the opening of the day. The view was so vast that tourist shops, hotels and cafés along the rim were nothing. Only the slender shardic layers near the very top of the canyon corresponded to human history. Where did the Anthropocene start, I wondered. A centimetre?

The light brought colour with it. Halfway down, the sun-touched rocks formed the contours of castles, each geometric shape part of a distinct type of rock system. By the time the sun hit the red in rocks forged hundreds of millions of years ago, still aeons from reaching the past of the canyon floor, it was glowing, burnished morning.

The flutter of dawn elk was still with us when we drove south into the smaller Oak Creek Canyon, the road winding steeply down an hour south of Flagstaff. First it was all ponderosa forests, but soon we were deep between red rock and blazes of red and yellow fall oaks. Later I would read Nicole Walker's book about Arizona and family and climate change and ponderosa and lilacs and joy, in which she writes of this drive into Oak Creek Canyon as itself being 'geological and, therefore, perspective making'. We descended into the slit of the canyon, a layered chasm formed by the slow, persistent flow of snow-melt. Snow-melt that is decreasing year by year. The bright foliage we drove through was newly thin, 21,000 acres of it having burnt in 2014's wildfires.

We met Walker and other writers from this place at the conference in Phoenix we'd participated in, Phoenix of course turning out to be much more than an airport hotel. Walker wrote of how every spring and fall she and her husband created a 'defensible space' around their Flagstaff home – and talked about moving to Portland, where it rains. She also wrote about the problem of metaphor and the difficulty we have in imagining other points of view, or imagining things as other from how they are – or, more vitally, as they *could* be. And, she wrote about Oak Creek Canyon, how it is part of the largest contiguous ponderosa pine forest in the United States, and how from a certain position at the top 'you can see waves of ponderosa forest stretching as long as the sea'. She wondered how many fires it would take for the forest to be no longer contiguous. When I read this I thought, this, here, is her ocean. Then I wondered what it felt like to be a tree, or an elk, in a forest that is like an ocean.

And when that ocean is on fire.

We slept in a shadowed cabin right down there in it.

The next afternoon we drove the few miles on down the road to Slide Rock, a natural 25-metre-long water slide worn into the flat red sandstone at the bottom of Oak Creek Canyon. It was what we'd been waiting for: one of the 'Top 10 swimming spots in the United States', according to a list we'd come across online. It was a human-sized canyon.

The water was truly freezing this time, 40–45 degrees Fahrenheit the park ranger at the entrance to the park told us. That's 4–5 degrees Celsius. That's colder than Lake Taupō in winter, cold enough to meet the International Ice Swimming Association's definition of cold.

There were other groups around on the slippery flat red rocks, but there were only four others swimming: a lone woman, and a man and his two teenage sons. Lena and Natasha paddled for a while in the bitter shallows and then it was time.

I went first, initially simply falling over on the rocks. A particular algae makes them slippery. The trick, it seemed, was to sit and let yourself go. When I did this, I was pulled into the steep narrow channel about a metre wide, and instantly the current was taking me.

When I managed to turn my head, I saw Lena had followed and had been pulled around. She was coming down behind me fast, headfirst, her face pushed under the water close to the rocky sides. I screamed and tried to stop myself, but I kept slipping, being pulled on in my own current. Things slowed down. Water rushed around me, Lena's head just out of reach.

The rock was gravelly and slick against my feet. I managed to splay my toes against both sides, and I caught her. I had her. But her body was slippery and heavy, and I couldn't get her out and I was slipping again. It was her screaming this time.

Then Tim was there, on the dry rock to the side. I got my footing and pushed her struggling body into his arms.

'We've got you, love, we've got you.'

I hardly knew who was saying it, Tim or me. But we had her. Safe and held.

Then Natasha slammed into me and we were both going down, and quickly we were pitched into a freezing pool, fear transformed into a flush of exhilaration, as if there was something in the water. Which there was: cold. My whole body tingled with the shock of it, my breath coming fast, adrenaline pumping through me.

I pushed this daughter, too, safely up to Tim on the flat rocks, and then, although it seems almost outlandish now, given how afraid Lena had been and I for her, I went on.

I bumped down another rapid, paused in the next pool, then let go again. It was faster this time, a real slide, at one point too narrow for my woman's hips so I became wedged in place, my head just above water, the stream rushing round me. Then I was through, the water pushing me so I plummeted into a deep cold pool that seemed bottomless, my head going under as I dropped. For a moment, the chill of the snow-fed water clamped me in its grip.

When I finally surfaced, I saw that Lena and Natasha were running along beside me, shouting words I couldn't make out. It turned out this one was my swim. It was joyous, then, to be this woman, this mother, this partner in this precise passing moment in the world's turns, muddy and bruised and reckless, my heart calling in warm blood to pump my core organs, my skin rising in rough goosebumps in response to the water. I was as immersed in it as I could ever be. I was alive.

The current slackened as the channel became wider and I floated on my back, moving on the flow like an insect carried by water, a daughter flying down either side, one blue and silver, the other blue and red, soaring from rock to rock.

We could have flown as easily as we swam. We could have spoken ibis.

When I reached a slow-moving open pool, both daughters ventured in again to join me, swimming swiftly, and Tim came in too. All around, the water flowed on, running around us and through us. Canyon cliffs rose up into an as yet untold future, the leaves turning and turning in their still annual red and yellow glory. Together for our breath of time, in the blazing cold of the canyon, we floated.

Pods

Cottesloe Beach Dissolves

My older brother, Matt, and I stood shining wet from a swim in the Indian Ocean. We were watching Lena and Natasha and his daughter, Katya, just a year younger than my girls, play in the waves. His son, Max, a high-octane six, was digging in the sand further up the beach beside Sonya.

'Davai, Maxy, davai,' I heard my sister-in-law murmuring to my nephew.

Come on, Maxy.

I'd missed hearing that. It had been nearly two years since they moved away.

Sonya and Max had picked Lena and Natasha and me up from the airport when we arrived, handing us ice-blocks as we got into the furnace of their car. Tim hadn't joined us on this trip, staying behind to work. It was October and cold in Wellington, but Perth was that kind of luxurious hot that makes your muscles unstitch, while still far from the scorching heat of the summer months we'd heard about.

My one request for the visit had been for a spectacular Western Australian beach. The teaching semester had almost finished and marking hadn't yet come in. My year of attending rudimentary reo Māori classes in the evenings was also almost over. I needed a holiday. Cottesloe delivered. Its sand and blue sea seemed to stretch forever, going on for hundreds of miles right up the coast.

The ease of the three girl cousins slipping through the water reminded me of my brother and me on the beach as kids. The water itself shimmered with memory. It was hard to remember this was a whole other ocean. Matt was nine when Tom was born, and I was six, so for a long time it was just the two of us. We learnt to swim in the sea in Auckland. For a moment, this standing together in the water felt like the latest snapshot, a still: brother and sister, back to camera, knee-deep in the sea (could be any sea), while a little way off their children play. If it were film, there'd be little dialogue – just one of those shots where people look happy and which is used to show the passage of time and to establish a new location.

The feeling I'm trying to find the words and stories for felt more liquid than that, though. It was like swimming underwater amid surf and stirred up sand, when you know what you're looking at but can't get orientated, shapes disappearing in the moment they're glimpsed, entangled shells and seaweed tumbling by. Seeing my brother and his family and this place they now live – and what relation all this bears to me – I ended up thinking about Uber rides and migrations, Rio Tinto and vegetarianism, and pods of embryos and whales.

I'd gone for a run alone along the bank of the Swan River on my first morning. Already there was the smell of mown grass, and the sight of outlandish Australian birds: a large sheeny raven, its harsh cawing somehow deliberate and human-seeming, and a pelican gulping something into its gullet. I'd paused to rest near a clutch of black shags with their wings out to dry beside the water, arrested by the black shine of their spreading feathers. As always, the run had begun to ground me. But it was also as though a dam on another part of life had been opened, and images from other visits with Matt, in the nearly thirty years since he left home, were streaming in.

There were all those Auckland flats of his I'd navigated to in the nineties with maps our grandfather sketched on the backs of envelopes. There were glimpses of Matt's visit to me at graduate school in the US, when I was so homesick I didn't know if I could make it through. There were the islands of visits to at least four crowded London flats he'd lived in when he was working in the film industry there. I remembered the time we went to a club and got a night bus home, and how glad I was to leave the group of his friends I didn't know, glad for it just to be the two of us sitting side by side at the front of the double-decker hurtling through the bright London night. In these passing dissolves, he's still very much the big brother, there looking out for me.

We'd done our first grown-up travel together, too, heading to London, then India because both of us had some of our earliest memories there, grafted at least in my case onto photographs of our parents in flared jeans holding one of us each. The latest film my brother produced had an Indian plot line where a New Zealand teenager goes AWOL and her estranged parents have to set off in search of her.

More recent visits had been different, with whole new currents.

There was Matt awkwardly holding one of my daughters as a baby. This was overlaid in my mind with an image of him at nine holding Tom in our parents' bedroom on the night our brother was born, not yet bathed and still disturbingly red and wet with goo from our mother's body. This was joined in turn by a memory of me pushing his baby daughter in a buggy, taking her away to a park to give him and Sonya a chance to sleep.

Paused in my run on that Perth riverbank, it was hard to comprehend how little of my daily mental space any of this history now took up, especially the pre-children times. But seen together, these sibling visits over the years emerged like part of a grammar, like the conjunctions structuring a specific syntax within a life.

Or like a rock formation, persistently appearing and disappearing with the tides.

And then, in a kind of jump-cut, this new faraway city, Perth, to be entered into.

The four cousins didn't seem to have been aware of any temporal ellipses. Direct from the airport, they'd joined together into a tight knot of play, deep in Beyblades and Twister and highly competitive rounds of Connect 4. We'd easily merged into a mass of family, my brother's life and my own all mixed up together again.

On the second day Sonya and I and the kids had swum in their small apartment-complex pool while Matt was at work, the Canning Highway humming in the background but visually fenced off. As the six of us cruised around in the water together, two mothers with two children apiece, I remembered how easily we sometimes parented together. When I scooped up my nephew from a second dive into the deep end, despite his not being able to swim, I felt a small tug that he wasn't my boy. It was more real, suddenly, because Tim and I were making decisions about the remaining embryos, gender unknown, from the IVF cycle by which we'd conceived our daughters.

Watching those awkwardly dancing birds on my run, and reeling through all those other visits to my brother, I was struck anew by the restless dispersal of my close family – both brothers living overseas, parents constantly moving house. It was a restlessness I shared in some way and was perhaps part of why I was struggling with being in one place so long: same city, same house, same job. Was I becoming the sister who went home? Thoroughly drying off her wings? Was this it?

What scared me more about being so placed was the risk

of becoming unable to imagine different lives, of my thoughts turning into narrow channels. Or perhaps I was just afraid of my life seeming to lack a story – at least from the outside.

I stood beside my brother, looking out at the sea from this latest beach.

Rio Tinto Naturescapes

I'd requested window seats. I wanted to see how it felt as that expanse of red earth, Australia, passed by beneath, remembering how it was after Arizona, when we saw the blueness of the sea. This seemed like part of what Perth must be – one of the most isolated cities in the world, a city built between the desert and the ocean. It was a seven-hour flight from Auckland. As it turned out, the flight path took us mainly across water, and the girls and I were glued to screens anyway. The only lead-in to our arrival was the generic long-haul flight.

We drove from the airport to the apartment, along wide flat roads flanked by the malls and dry-country trees of southern Perth. We could have been almost anywhere in Australia, or in California.

The apartment was like many of the places Matt and his family had rented in recent years in Auckland: cream carpets, white walls, breakfast bar, well-designed rooms with functional storage.

They didn't really fit my image of economic migrants, but there was no question they had left Auckland for better work, more affordable housing, a walk to school, an easier commute, more time with their children. My brother's job in film development was more exciting and stable than anything he'd had in Auckland for a long time. For a while there, things had been tough. His and Sonya's contract work was always precarious and they seemed to have to give up their rented homes on a semi-annual basis when the owners sold, eager for an injection of capital gain. The worst was when they'd had to move between the day Sonya went into hospital to give birth, and when she came home with a newborn.

They were among the approximately 25,000 New Zealanders who moved to Australia in 2018. But then, almost the same number of Australians moved across the Tasman the other way that year. All these people seeking something else, somewhere else. This was before the fires that made many New Zealanders in Australia start talking about coming home if they could, and a whole existence before both countries closed their borders.

After the weekend, Matt went back to work and that morning the rest of us set out for Kings Park. Lena and Natasha wrestled on the kerb while I waited with them for an Uber, too many of us to fit in Matt and Sonya's car. The three of us had woken well before dawn and the girls giggled on the grass in the brittle, tired way I knew could end in fingernails and pinching.

'Looks like trouble,' the driver said as I got into the front, the girls jostling to be the first to climb into the back seat.

I laughed my agreement.

Dealing with their bickering and occasional moments of actual cruelty had turned out to be one of the most distressing parts of parenting.

The driver swiped at his phone and said we'd need to divert. There were protests in the city centre.

'Is it Extinction Rebellion?' I asked. I turned to Lena and Natasha in the back. 'We could join the protests later, girls,' I said, trying to distract them.

It sounded as if I was proposing a jolly picnic, something out of Enid Blyton.

They didn't respond. They'd gone quiet and shy in the car with someone they didn't know. My comment was partly meant for the driver, anyway, and they probably knew it. It was a performance of a sort. I was testing the waters, pushing; something I found I wanted to do more and more on questions of how we were collectively managing our world. There had been a shift in the prevailing mood and I was working out, interaction by interaction, how I wanted to move within it. The girls were working things out too, feeling their way around what it was 'our family' did and believed, and how other people might believe different things.

The man shrugged, waving towards the map showing our new route to Kings Park. 'This way we can avoid them.'

Best for him to avoid talking politics if he was to sidestep arguments with riders. It was his car, anyway.

We drove across the western bridge of the Swan River, the river opening out so wide it felt like the harbour itself, the city on one side, its arterial southern suburbs on the other. In the 1890s, the limestone reef at the mouth of the river not far off, near Fremantle, was blasted away, turning what had been a freshwater system into a tidal estuary.

The city skyline was built along the north side of the river, like in Melbourne and Adelaide. I could see what Matt had talked about on the phone after they'd first moved – there was Rio Tinto, its red block characters on the tallest building. In the Pilbara region up north, Rio Tinto runs the biggest iron ore production centre in the world. Woodside was on another building – the largest operator of oil and gas in Australia. And there was BHP Billiton. It was featured in a *Guardian* article we'd both read about the twenty fossil fuel companies whose exploitation of world oil, gas and coal reserves could be linked directly to more than a third of all greenhouse gas emissions in the modern era. Matt and I had talked about the article while making breakfast toast for the kids.

After a silence I asked the driver, 'You from here?'

'Yep, lived in Perth my whole life.'

Must be complicated, I thought. Or not. I didn't push it further. Perth's fortunes are directly linked to these companies.

Matt had flipped through TV news channels before heading into the office, talking about how housing prices had plummeted since the 2014 peaks of the latest mining boom. There were constant stories of families with negative equity, their mortgages more than their houses were worth. Many of them were former fly-in-fly-out workers, having lost lucrative work in the industry. It was good for renters new to town, though. Housing like Matt and Sonya's was there for the taking. And the city centre still felt wealthy to us whenever we went downtown. Everyone thought things would bounce back. Australia had just had their climate change election: it seemed the majority had decided not to worry, so had re-elected Scott Morrison. He'd promised to protect the role of fossil fuels in Australia's 'energy future'; he had brought a lump of coal into parliament as a kind of totem of that promise. 'This is coal,' he'd said. 'Don't be afraid.'

'Shall I take you to the main entrance to the park?' the driver asked.

'I think so,' I said, 'We're aiming for the nature playground place. It's named for one of the mining companies.'

'Rio Tinto Naturescape,' he replied helpfully.

I glanced across but detected no hint of implied commentary.

Matt had described it as 'a cheap bit of green-washing'. 'But it's a good playground,' he'd said. 'Katya and Max love it. It's all natural wood structures.'

Lena and Natasha would love it too, I was sure.

The man dropped us off at the park entrance, a short walk from the playground he said. We wandered out onto a promontory while we waited for the others and looked down over the river and the city. Lena and Natasha had formed a close unit again and drifted together to look at the Eternal Flame of Remembrance, part of the State War Memorial. The structure was in the centre of a shallow pool of blue water, the small orange flicker uncanny in the daylight. The girls balanced along the edge of the pool and Natasha wanted to know if the flame was really *really* eternal.

'Not much is eternal,' I said.

Standing looking out at the city skyline, I hoped not. I hoped this version of civilisation wouldn't be forever. But that felt like a cruel thing to say to my children.

'Probably Indigenous Australian peoples had their own flames here,' I said instead, 'for much longer. It would have been a good place for a campfire.'

More than 47,000 years of campfires even. *That* seemed like eternity. This flame had been here since 2000.

The oldest pieces of Earth's crust on the planet's surface are in Western Australia, over four billion years old. At Pilbara, further north where the Rio Tinto mine is, the rocks are nearly three and a half billion years old.

In the early mornings, when we woke before light, I'd been reading *Benang: From the Heart*, a novel by Perth-born Noongar writer Kim Scott. An Australian colleague had lent it to me before I left Wellington. It was proving hard to stop thinking about. Scott's novel was based on his own family history and sought to find a way to tell the story of the murder and violent removal of his people from their land at the end of the nineteenth and beginning of the twentieth centuries. Of their confinement into 'settlements', 'reserves', 'missions', 'refugee camps', 'holding pens' – and of the systematic taking of their children as part of State-sponsored assimilation programmes. Scott wrote, too, about the arrival of times of 'great explosions', when it first began to rain 'earth and mallee roots and small dead animals'.

The pain of it made me newly aware of the sheer difference in scale between the period of human history in this place before colonisation – invasion – compared with the period after. I'd felt this shock before in Australia.

The girls and I were still hovering around the eternal flame.

The term 'solastalgia', coined by Australian environmental philosopher Glenn Albrecht in 2005, seemed too luxurious a word for the sense of dispossession and loss that must be felt here. But I grasped for it to help me towards the smallest inkling of the grief. I thought of the bare hillsides in Aotearoa, cleared, in some cases by my own ancestors, of the trees and birds and people who once lived there, forcing them elsewhere – or nowhere at all. Solastalgia comes from the terms 'solace' and 'desolation'. It is an effort to describe the intense desolation felt in a landscape that, at one time deeply known by those who lived there, has been transformed in such a way that it no longer provides solace.

I remembered a talk I'd heard Sydney-based novelist James Bradley give about climate crisis, where he'd responded to a question about the best books to read to understand what was coming next. He said to read books by Indigenous Australian authors like Alexis Wright, a member of the Waanyi Nation, because for them the apocalypse has already happened. Someone in the audience challenged him on why he thought things were so bad. I remembered her height and the tightness of her voice. Why was he so pessimistic? the woman asked. Surely it wasn't that bad? He was gracious in his response, in particular to the details she gave of what her own community was trying to do in the region of the Great Barrier Reef, but he held firm to the argument that things were not fine, and were not all going to be all right.

Lena and Natasha were by now high up a tree. I looked up the location of the playground on my phone. It was close and it promised to be 'a place for children to connect with nature and learn to appreciate the unique Western Australian environment'. The playground even had a philosophy, arising from the concern that urban kids were becoming 'disconnected from the natural world'. This concern, according to the playground website, led to the question: *'How can we expect children to care for something they have never experienced?'* Their italics, not mine. This was followed by the sentence: 'Rio Tinto Naturescape Kings Park delivers a practical response to this issue.'

With half an eye on how high my girls were climbing in the tree near the flame, I googled 'Extinction Rebellion Perth' instead. It was a relief to see images of people staging a sit-in right then in the middle of a busy intersection downtown. I paused on a photo of a middle-aged figure in red, their soft face painted mime-white, eyes blackened. They faced a white police horse in a black bridle and stretched out a hand as if to stroke the creature's neck. They looked defiantly unafraid. A placard read: *Respect Existence or Expect Resistance.*

Not long ago I would have seen these people as utterly different from me. They were enacting a different kind of radicalism, one that had little to do with the daily life I knew. Now they seemed like one of the few sane things around.

Geography Lesson III

Sonya and I were standing either side of the breakfast bar in the kitchen, discussing dinner. She was making chicken udon for her kids and a surimi salad for her and Matt, and we were figuring out what the vegetarian versions of these would be. Matt had called from work and suggested rice balls for us, which I reckoned we could all just have, but that wasn't how it was going to work. The first meal had been carefully fitted to our needs, and the next night I'd cooked, but by now we had been around a few days.

Sonya asked, 'But what do you eat?'

I had to think for a bit.

'Lots of curries,' I said. 'Noodles. Tofu. Lots of beans, I guess. Hummus . . .'

Chicken went in with the noodles. Crab meat with the broccoli and eggs, with some left out for us. I made my own salad, assembled finger food for the girls, who were tucked up on the sofa watching a movie with their cousins, then sat down on the other side of the bar with a second beer.

I liked that she'd asked why we were vegetarian (we'd had some version of this conversation a number of times), and why we'd now stopped eating even fish, which we'd eaten the last time they saw us.

'Climate change,' I said, and lapsed into a list. 'The dairy industry. Animals. Big industry fishing. All that. There was this

George Monbiot article . . .'

I liked her curiosity. It was genuine – she wasn't the choir, and there was something appealing about this, perhaps for my brother as well. In fact, my brother wasn't the choir either, but that seemed harder for me to recognise. There's a tendency with family members to see what we share rather than what differs.

I tried to remember what about the Monbiot piece had clinched it for me, but I could only remember how the piece started with the general collapse of life in the oceans, primarily from fishing. Maybe what made the difference was that the evening Tim and I read the piece we met a woman at a party who had also read it, and we agreed together we should stop. We tried to avoid the language of 'giving up' something; it sounded too virtuous, too much like Lent.

'I used to say it wasn't that important to me,' I told Sonya now. 'I'd say that I didn't care what other people did.'

I used to be more polite.

Perhaps I was still too polite.

But then I saw, also, how I was haranguing her, sitting there with my beer as she tried to cook three different dinners, slicing greasy chicken on the chopping board. Something had slipped off-balance. At the same time there felt like a necessary openness between us. We faced each other across the counter, the children's sounds only a background murmur now. I found I wanted to force it, but I knew I wasn't going to win.

'I've always hated milk,' she said, 'and we're eating less red meat. But *fish*. I grew up on fish.'

When she was growing up, she told me, her mother had a dacha where she managed to grow a few – very few – vegetables. Besides that, they had fresh fish. 'That's why we were okay in the nineties,' she said, 'when it was so hard for everyone.'

It was often like this, I remembered. For a while we'd pretend we had the same expectations, the same culture. I pretended I was the challenging one. I knew about queerness and feminism and the environment. Then the terrain would shift, and the geography Sonya carried with her, that I simply couldn't know, jutted into view.

She's younger than me, so would have still been a child in the nineties. I remembered news footage of people in Russia queuing for bread. It must have been shown often enough – and explained often enough by my parents, even if they tried to signal that it oversimplified things – to have stuck. I think I was meant to realise that things weren't that great under communism either.

'I wouldn't give up fish,' Sonya said.

These days her mother grew flowers in that same dacha to sell to children who took them to celebrate the first day of the school year. And it was still hard.

I watched Sonya squeeze rice balls for my family. She'd always been stylish – beautiful, in fact. Her heavy-rimmed glasses, which had once seemed intriguingly Soviet, were the current trend here too. If the world was divided between us, she'd got glamour, an outfit even for the beach. She'd worn a white blazer to the playground. I'd enjoyed it when a couple of years ago she'd asked me if I was dyeing my hair grey. Some of her friends in Moscow were doing it. She'd also got the outside perspective of someone who had been brave enough to move her life across the world.

She repeated, with new emphasis, 'I couldn't give fish up.'

I think I just nodded.

And I wouldn't eat it, either. Although, I did eat eggs and butter and copious amounts of cheese.

Their dacha was in Magadan, where Sonya grew up at the seaport in Northern Siberia. The nearest city accessible by road, Yakutsk, is as far away as Adelaide is from Perth. Magadan is a mining town like Perth, but fly-in-fly-out work is something different in a subarctic climate. Many of the men she and Matt talked about there did this kind of work. Most of the year the ground is frozen.

When she and my brother went back to Magadan with Katya as a baby, the men made Matt swim in the frozen sea.

'Hard to imagine you'd end up in Perth, right?' I half joked, feebly.

But she didn't seem to think she'd 'ended up' here, or 'ended up' anywhere. Where they would be next year was an open question. 'There's always so much about your life I don't know,' I said.

She'd moved from Magadan to Vladivostok to work in shipping logistics, and she and Matt met at a film festival there. I didn't know what shipping logistics meant either, even when she did the same work in Auckland, but I imagined her peering at bright screens, charting complex movements of goods around the globe, the screens themselves like high-tech fish tanks. It was an image that always had her looking outwards to other places. Matt had already been learning Russian for years when they met. He studied Russian literature at university, while she studied English literature. He returned to Russia for another visit, she visited Auckland, and then she moved – although it wasn't as simple as that sounds, either emotionally or bureaucratically. Only in the weeks of their moving together from Auckland to Australia had she finally become a New Zealand citizen, and that was touch and go. Years earlier, when Katya was a baby still being breastfed, for a few weeks it looked possible that the New Zealand state would send Sonya back to Russia, and the Russian state not let her daughter in.

I'd had thoughts about how Sonya wasn't keen on spending another summer in Perth. She wanted to move home to Auckland. That was impractical, I'd thought, given Matt's work situation. Those earlier thoughts of mine seemed ungenerous now. To my brother too.

Part of what Sonya had time to do, while she wasn't working over here, was keep Katya's and Max's Russian up. Their household runs largely in Russian, and I was so used to this I hardly thought about it. The children's written Russian was as good as their English, their little workbooks set up for them to do homework every morning before school. At one point, Sonya had trained as a teacher. Until that moment in the kitchen over dinner, I hadn't got much further than noticing the order of this household in comparison to my own – as though they were simply two comparable units of space and people. I'd hardly thought about what teaching her children must mean to her, especially given her parents and sister don't speak English.

When her father, Nikolai, came to Auckland there'd been a lot of smiling and nodding within our extended family. It was uncanny to see my brother joking in Russian with his father-in-law. The two of them – men in a family of women – were close, and at Christmas dinner they leaned back in their chairs, beers in hand, faces creased in laughter, my brother both familiar and an entirely different man. I'd had a similar jolt the first evening in Perth on seeing Matt dressed from work, the public sector exec in ironed shirt and black suede shoes.

On that visit it became Nikolai's task to pick up his grandchildren, which required a long walk along busy North Shore roads. On his first pick-up day alone, he got lost on the way to school, and called Sonya at work. All she could tell, she later said, was that he was in the middle of a traffic island somewhere. He couldn't read the signs or ask for help, and she didn't yet know the area well enough to direct him, to move him remotely as she might manoeuvre ships towards the right shipping lanes. Perhaps she could hear the vibrating hum of traffic, like the motor of a distant boat you can hear when underwater. She told the story as a funny anecdote but she talked, too, about the panic in her father's voice.

Six months after Matt and Sonya moved to Perth, Nikolai died suddenly in Magadan. Sonya and Katya made it in time for the funeral. I could only try to imagine.

*

Dinner was ready, the movie finished, my brother home.

Sonya came around from the kitchen side of the bench, which in the moment seemed like the helm of a small vessel, and we laid the table together.

Pods

Natasha, Lena and I were wrapped up in blankets against the wind on a boat. At first it seemed we weren't going to see much. The air was filled with the chatty voiceover of a woman who kept talking about how their boat had built a relationship with the whales, how the whales had learnt to trust her and had become curious about her. It all seemed both appealing and implausible – as if the whales *liked* us watching them.

The boat moved further out on the slightly choppy waters from Fremantle, where we'd visited the weekend markets, and the passengers settled down on the decks to wait. There were about forty of us, Australians and 'foreign' tourists alike in sandals and windbreakers.

We headed in the direction of Rottnest Island, Wadjemup in the Noongar language, which during the last ice age was part of the mainland, accessible on foot. It only became cut off when global sea levels rose as the polar ice caps melted again, seven to nine thousand years ago. I'd read that oral histories, astoundingly, told of the time before, when Wadjemup was an important meeting place. In what moment did the stories declare it an island, I wondered, and when did the walk become an impossible swim, the water rising from ankle to knee to neck to throat?

The island had been used for almost a century from 1838 as a site of Aboriginal incarceration and forced labour. Some prisoners had been hanged there. This hadn't stopped it becoming a popular holiday destination.

Lena and Natasha were quiet, watching the sea for signs of life. The boat rocked as it moved slowly further from shore.

Then, after a time that seemed much shorter than we'd anticipated, among the waves about 100 metres away, a small whale made a crescent as it surfaced followed by the bulk of its mother. One ... two, one ... two, they crested in turn, each breaching the surface of the water almost sleepily, before disappearing, crescent moons rising and setting in the water.

The pair seemed more intent on their own doings than curious about us. Maybe the ferry to Rottnest had woken them and now the calf wanted to feed. I remembered what having a baby woken was like. There was an intimacy about the whales' lazy movements, but they stayed their distance, and then disappeared altogether.

After that, not much happened for a while. The three of us went down into the cabin, almost below sea level, and the girls got me to read to them. I thought they were simply finding the book exciting, with its demons and fairies and the brave brother and sister working together to defeat evil. Who wouldn't want to imagine such a world? But perhaps their insistence I read whenever we were alone was also about returning to the intimacy of the three of us – of getting back their mother's full attention.

On a seat nearby a woman burped and vomited discreetly into a plastic bag. Her husband was silent but close beside her. The boat rocked gently. I read on. A young woman, pretty with her hair in a bun and pale tattooed arms with swirled lines right down to vulnerable wrists, stroked her partner's long hair as she lay back on the cabin floor, eyes closed. Natasha looked pale too, almost grey. We started to wonder when we could go back. We were done. We'd seen our whale.

But that wasn't it.

We'd been out nearly an hour and a half when the crew announced they'd sighted a pod of three large males.

'I thought a pod was a whole group,' Lena commented, as we headed upstairs to stare again at what looked like empty sea.

I had too. But a pod, it turned out, could be as small as two whales. The term simply means a group formed through biological connection, or through friendship. A pod might be together for a day or for months. Our loudspeaker guide told us there were stories of the same whales meeting up year after year to swim together along stretches of their migration.

Lena's comment made me realise I hadn't really expected to see more than one or two whales. The solitude of the single southern right whale, the tohorā, in Wellington Harbour in the winter the year before had seemed, well, normal. Now I saw the stark solitariness of a whale alone in an ocean. The term 'rare' signalled that kind of solitude as well. I'd read a piece by Harriet Riley on 'endlings', a term first used in *Nature* in 1996 for an animal that is the last of its species. I was reading ecologically focused writing with my students that semester, and together we'd also encountered the term 'Eremocene', the age of loneliness. It felt far more resonant than the Anthropocene, the age of humans. The age of loneliness affected us all.

But loneliness wasn't a problem for these humpbacks. Since hunting was stopped in the 1960s the population, thought to have dropped to as low as 450, had recovered. Our loudspeaker guide told us that as many as 25,000 humpbacks migrate annually now, which is close to the estimates of pre-1900 populations. This felt like an unlikely good news environmental story, a much-needed tale of having found a way to inhabit a space together without one group displacing another.

At first, the pod of three whales was just glimpses of grey in the distance while our boat tried to find its rhythm of plunge and rise. Once we found their measure, we were able to move so we were right alongside each time they surfaced after an underwater streak. The three of them swam in parallel to one another, taking turns rising, just breaching the surface of the water, then going beneath again with a great fluid tail flick. One ... two ... three ... one ... two ... three. Each time a fluke turned upwards it briefly revealed an underside of white.

As we motored south alongside them, our guide told us that the whales would have been swimming down beside these sand beaches for weeks, from the warm north of the Kimberley region at the top of Western Australia where the calving areas are, towards the feeding grounds around Antarctica. I thought I could see Cottesloe in the distance, where we'd swum a few days before. It felt different now, knowing that whales swam out here.

The three males arrived in the quiet waters protected by the island. Then it seemed there was movement everywhere. Ahead of us, another cow and her calf surfaced. Then off to the right, another. The mothers don't eat for the six months of the migration, getting skinnier and skinnier as their calves grow. We watched the closest grey female rise, then change her course abruptly, going for us, right under the boat. We waited nervously, wondering if she was big enough to topple us. The minute stretched. Then she surfaced and was right there beside us, followed by her calf, the smaller creature metres long and studded with growths of barnacles. They were each a whole ecology. We heard the sighed exhalation of the mother's breath.

I thought of the grandeur of the elk at dawn at the Grand Canyon – its casual observation, then its dismissal of us, its breath misting up the morning air.

My class and I had also read an essay by the Perth writer Rebecca Giggs, from the book she was then working on, *Fathoms:*

The World in the Whale. She'd cautioned against the 'self-satisfied' story of the humpbacks' recovery, with its emphasis on a human capacity for benevolence and awe, and on the ultimate resilience of another species. We were drawn, she said, to the myth of whales' 'remarkable otherness, their strange, wondrous and vast animalian world'. We were. I was. It wasn't that I wanted to repeat this myth, though. I understood that admiring creatures and leaving them alone wasn't going to be enough for them to survive – or any of us. Whales, according to Giggs, were the most polluted animals on Earth, because of what they absorb from the sea over their long lifespans. About the same length as our own.

The woman on the loudspeaker was laughing in delight as she talked, reeling out facts about the whales and their habits. We were an hour late and the crew were completely engrossed in the chase. Below deck, the woman was still spewing, her vertigo harder to cope with as we went further overtime, the crew not quite able to conceive this wasn't bliss for everyone.

But all around us, beneath the water, beyond where we could see, my daughters and I felt fleetingly able to imagine the lives of pod upon pod of whales.

These waters flowed between the whole Australian continent and the now separate land fragment before the open ocean. Later, I read that Wadjemup (Rottnest) is considered by its traditional owners, the Whadjuk Noongar people, to be a place of transition between the physical and spiritual worlds. Spirits travel to Wadjemup on their journey towards the afterlife; when a spirit is ready to leave our physical world, it travels across to the west of the island – towards the setting sun – and from there a whale carries the spirit on.

After we returned home to Wellington, I sought out footage of whales and listened to the whistles and grunts that made up the males' songs, the longest and most complex rhythmic syntax in the non-human animal world. One whale would take a song from another and return it with a new rhythm of its own. Humpbacks pass song fragments across hundreds of miles. I wondered what those songs sounded like when humpbacks met again after a gap of time. What sounds did they make to acknowledge and guide one another? I watched the footage again and again, wanting to see the way even the most enormous adult whale appeared weightless as he soared through the water, the way a calf slept on its mother's back, and the way one whale's long white throat grooves curved and stretched, concertina-like as, remaking grace, they leapt, from water into air.

And when I thought of the pods of whales in the weeks that followed, I thought also of my brother's marriage, and of the fluid families we all inhabit, broad and strange. I thought about my family and my brother's family, and how these pods would continue to reform in different ways over the decades, whatever shapes they took, swimming together for a portion of the migrations our respective movements followed.

Even as I work over these recent memories, I am aware of my lean away from conflict towards reconciliation, both in relationships and in writing, and how that can mean I only tell part of the story. But after we returned home it felt as though the whales swam inside me, pushing outwards and creating enough volume for multiple ways of being in the world, for multiple grammars and songs, the evolution of myriad co-existing routes. It seemed possible there could be ways to inhabit this planet together, all of us swimming in the same brine. Those of us who were left.

I remembered sitting on the sofa with Matt and Sonya on our last night. All our kids were in bed, and they were up to the final episode of the Netflix docuseries *Living Undocumented*, so we watched it together. Then we talked about New Zealand films my brother had made me watch fifteen years ago, telling me I 'had to check them out' and 'these people are going somewhere'. This was the good stuff. He was right, although *Tongan Ninja* still mystifies me. We surfed through old trailers.

Finally comfortable enough, or with just enough breathing space, I started to talk about the process Tim and I were going through to donate the embryos from our IVF cycle. We'd been unfathomably lucky – a single embryo gave us our two daughters, splitting into two identical collections of cells in the moment it was placed inside my body. This was the modern world too, and I was glad of it. The whales had made me think of those extra embryos – extra, beyond our needs – floating in a petri dish, each microscopic collection of seven or eight cells containing potential life, as simultaneously small and momentous as a single whale in an ocean. It was almost impossible, the knowledge that what became our own daughters, flicking out limbs inside my own watery body, once floated in that shared brine. I thought of the other meaning of pod – a vessel that carries a plant's seeds before dispersal.

I sat on the end of my brother's sofa in Perth, my feet tucked up under me and a cup of tea in my hands, and told them about sitting with Tim in a counsellor's office a few months before, and about how, when the woman to whom we were considering giving these embryos walked into the room and sat alone on a chair opposite us, I felt a tremor of recognition at her Russian accent. That moment was what had formed the bridge, making me for the first time see that I might be able to say yes, I could do this thing. I hadn't been sure until then, while Tim was always more certain we could. The sense of recognition resonated with both familiarity and distance, intimacy and difference, family and something utterly other. It evoked both care and space. Which felt right. It was an unanticipated pleasure, the way in which something so foreign, and still unequivocally challenging, could have become so much like family. And that family could carry so much of elsewhere. Whatever happens, the story felt like my gift to Sonya and my brother. Or theirs to me.

It was something to move on with.

Fossils

Sussex

Yet more remote,
Where the rough cliff hangs beetling o'er its base,
All breathes repose; the water's rippling sound Scarce heard;
but now and then the sea-snipe's cry [1]
Just tells that something living is abroad
—Charlotte Smith, *Beachy Head* (1806), lines 110–114

1. [Smith's note:] In crossing the channel this bird is heard at night, uttering a short cry, and flitting along near the surface of the waves.

We had only been in Britain a few hours, but this was the chilly kind of sea I knew. We walked through the streets of Shoreham-by-Sea to the shingle beach on the edge of the English Channel. The sky was a soft hazy blue. There was no one else there, just our small clutch of visiting extended family. Perhaps this was because all the beachgoers were along the coast in Brighton with its hot chips and brightly painted pier, or because the end of September was too late in the season for swimming, or perhaps this just wasn't one of the spots where people do what was once called 'sea-bathing'. It had been months since we'd swum in the sea.

The beach was strewn with strands of kelp which proved both slippery and sticky under our bare feet. The sea itself was choppy and awash with shells and sand, and it was immediately deep, the water pulling stones around our knees, a strong tug and push at our legs, so we held hands with the kids as we went in. All we did was get waist-deep and dip our heads under the water a couple of times, before dripping our way awkwardly back up over the grey stones.

Still, that must have been something like how they used to do it, when people began getting in the water here in the eighteenth and nineteenth centuries. A dip. I knew Sussex was one of the places in Europe where the practice first became popular. Swimming as bathing. Swimming as a brief but vital immersion in another element, considered beneficial for all sorts of ailments. A medicinal flush. Dunking the body in the natural world. A friend told me this is what Māori used to do too, although it killed many people when influenza came, the cold sea more danger than cure for a cough and sore chest.

But there we all were on the stony Sussex beach, true to the prescription, cold, wet and predictably happy, wrapped in towels, the grit of our plane and train journeys washed away.

Out of the water, but without my glasses on to focus things, I began to see ghostly shapes on the horizon. At first, we were unsure what they were and we asked each other, pointing out at the shapes rising like sea monsters from old maps. The last time I'd looked out at remote structures like that, off the coast of Taranaki, they'd turned out to be oil rigs. But these weren't oil rigs. Nor sea monsters. They were windmills.

I later did a search on the windmills, just to be sure, and saw that some were as far as 25 kilometres offshore. No wonder we could hardly make them out. The area was initially named Zone 6, but when it was completed a few months before we visited it had been renamed Rampion Offshore Wind Farm, for the county wildflower, the round-headed rampion or 'Pride of Sussex'. The small deep-blue flowers grow almost exclusively on the chalky grasslands of the Sussex South Downs. I found a description of them as seeming like 'a single bloom' but really being 'a collection of multiple smaller flower heads clustered together, slightly resembling a land-bound sea anemone'. Or a strange flowering windmill, I thought, with multiple blades.

Rampion Wind Farm felt like a hopeful sight in an isolationist, almost Brexit-era Britain, and not just for its promise of clean power generation. At its closest, Europe was hardly further away than those windmills. At that moment, it still seemed swimmable.

I imagined the *phit, phit, phit* of the windmill blades, knowing how immense they are up close, the stem-like body of each arm the length of a tennis court. They would vibrate in storms, blasted by huge swells, slick with water, the roar of the sea world all around them, tentacles swinging.

Sussex was different for me from the other places we swam on our travels. I felt that strongly as I sat on the shingle beach, aware of the Downs behind, the place itself tangibly part of the heterogeneous collection of experiences that made up my life. I only remembered swimming here once before, sometime in my twenties. I'd been picnicking with friends one afternoon among the crowds near the foot of Brighton Pier, music tinkling in a loop from the merry-go-round. I think we'd visited the folly that is the Georgian Brighton Pavilion. But I'd been living here in my head on and off for the past two decades, as well as occasionally being here in person. I'd walked this coast and I'd read about other women – and written about other women – walking it.

When sea-bathing first became a fashionable activity in the early eighteenth century, it was thought the colder the better. The winter months were regarded as the best time for a dip – 5am in January was ideal. That worked for Britain, I guess. I'd read the young novelist Frances Burney's accounts of going into the water here in a newly invented bathing machine, a kind of shed on wheels sometimes yoked to a horse designed to allow women to bathe modestly. She would have worn a long bathing gown (a few decades earlier she might have been naked) and been helped into the ice-cold water by one of the 'bathing-women' who administered the activity. This woman might possibly have also thrown a bucket of cold water over Burney's head. In 1773 Burney recorded in her journal that she found the shock of her first-ever sea 'plunge' at the age of twenty-one, prescribed for a persistent cold, 'terribly frightening', but that it left a 'glow that was delightful' – 'the finest feeling in the world'. After a decade of trips to the coast she wrote more tranquilly about bathing at dawn in November in the light of the moon, finding the ocean water 'cold but pleasant', and dressing by candlelight back at her room in a Brighton inn. She may have drunk a nice early morning glass of seawater to increase the health benefits of her dip. When I read this, I'd wondered how pleasant the cold water felt to the bathing-women, who could expect to stand waist-deep for hours on end under the moon as those human bodies were plunged in and out of the sea, and I hoped they too got some enjoyment from their role in the whole weird sadistic enterprise.

Swimming here felt a bit like dunking myself with Burney and those bathing-women, even while the peculiar practices associated with their immersions highlighted the myriad constraints placed on women's physical actions over the years, including swimming. And even if we were just here on a warmish late-autumn afternoon.

Looking out at this expanse of water on which remote windmills now turned, I felt I was also looking through eyes other than my own. Apart from Burney and the bathing-women, I thought of Sussex poet Charlotte Smith, who wrote of watching sea battles between Britain and France on almost this same horizon, and about the boats of refugees from Revolutionary France which began arriving in the freezing autumn of 1792 following the September massacres in Paris, when the revolution turned bloody. For the next ten years, it is estimated around twelve thousand émigrés from Europe arrived on this coast every year, some of them coming in open boats with little but the clothes they wore. Most wouldn't have been able to swim. How many of them drowned out there?

In 1792 Smith wrote a long poem, *The Emigrants*, about them. And in 2016, with a colleague from Melbourne, I was editing Smith's poem. The contemporary refugee crisis in Europe was continuing to escalate and the two situations became tangled in my mind.

Now I was sitting on the Sussex beach among a crowd of relatives, and it wasn't so much that I was miles away, as centuries. Or, at least, that different centuries were braided through one another.

It was twenty years since I had come to England to do a master's degree in eighteenth- and nineteenth-century British literature. Without much decision-making on my part, the fact that I was a reader and wrote decent assignments about books had transmuted, oddly, into that journey – to saying goodbye to my parents, who then still lived with my younger brother on the farm in the Wairarapa, and taking up a scholarship and a plane ticket out.

I wanted to make a real journey of it. I'd just been given the 1835 travel journal of a British ancestor named Augusta, and I decided to follow in her footsteps. So in the two months before I was due to show up at the University of York, I backpacked my way around parts of what was once the Austro-Hungarian Empire. Augusta had travelled with her Lancashire family of thirteen and a baby grand piano through Europe when she was twenty; her final journal entry in the single volume I had told of her engagement to an Austro-Hungarian count. It was all very much like a period novel, although Augusta never got to marry her count and went on to translate a history of Germany instead. I was twenty-three and kept a journal of my own. No piano, no family, fewer languages, less money, no engagements, but different opportunities.

Once I made it to York, Augusta's journal became the kernel of my thesis, which I titled 'Domesticity Abroad: An Analysis of Family Travel and Women's Travel Journals, 1814–1848'. The title now makes me laugh. Even then, had I *wanted* to have family here with me? To be away from home, but not alone? I don't think I was ever fully committed to the narrative of the great escape, of necessity solitary. At that stage I was mostly interested in daughters who were on the move. I hardly noticed their mothers.

On the beach I glanced over at my own children. They were at their very easiest when they had their hands busy with sand or stones on a beach, offering a rare stretch in which I was free to think.

Somehow, during that year living in a brick hostel in York, I'd also written a draft of my first proper book, interweaving Augusta's journey with my own in an effort to make something that would be part travel narrative, part love story, part history of women's travel. I was always more interested in messing up the past with the present than in treating literature more formally, as I'd been required to do in my thesis. I wanted to explore how we all swam in related waters. My book about Augusta also formed the template of most of the non-fiction I've written since: 'footsteps writing', in which I would approach the world through movement and enter it via literature, figuring out my own experiences through those of another, usually a dead other.

I'm now distant enough from my own earlier experience, too, to see that this approach shielded me in some way from writing the present. It was as though I needed backup – or, more accurately, foreground – to allow me to talk about the world. I wasn't fully confident in where to place myself within it.

The book of strange swimming explorations I'm writing now is in some way an attempt to remedy that, although as I lay on the beach in Sussex I had no idea I would write it. Like my first trip here to study, I'd made this visit to England on the strength of my identity as a literary scholar and Romanticist.

It took me nearly two decades to finish the long-delayed scholarly book about British women travellers which I'd begun at York. The intervening period included a doctorate in the US, where I read and wrote in converted army barracks in Princeton then in a flat in Brooklyn, a year in Berlin, a return home to Wellington, a first teaching job, a house, beginning a family of my own. By then, the book had become about women wanderers of all sorts, not just in travel writing but in sentimental fiction, gothic novels, epic poetry and sonnets. I wrote a lot about women who felt lost or homesick, and about those who had no home to return to. I wrote about loneliness and forms of *deep homelessness*. I wrote about the social conditions that produced such states, and about the moments when people feel adrift. I wrote about how these kinds of experiences produced, and perhaps were most effectively evoked by, what I called 'wandering texts' – narratives and verse without clear paths forward.

By the time I finished the book, I was beginning seriously to wonder what all this had to do with me. I wondered about it yet again as I lay on the beach with my family. But I had continued to be drawn to the ways these stories challenged narratives about travel (and life) as a great self-directed voyage out, an experiment in the discovery of the self. These women's movements (and lives) didn't play out like that. No more than did my own. Things turned out to be a lot messier, more random and often disorientating. This awareness continued to resonate, even after I'd lived in one house in Wellington for ten years. Especially after I'd lived in one house for ten years and become a mother.

And I was still a reader. I continued to be stirred by moments in novels and poems and travel books when forward momentum seemed paused, moments in which people found space to contemplate and feel the world outside themselves – sometimes by reading itself, or just by walking near the sea. It was those moments more than anything else, when anxiety and chatter momentarily dropped away, that I kept seeking.

The children were beginning to look chilly on the beach and I saw it was almost time to gather them up and head off to find dinner. But the other adults were still discussing the windmills and plans for the following days, and I was still being tugged at by my thoughts. It could wait a little longer.

Given how close I was to having decided I was no longer even interested in eighteenth- and nineteenth-century British writing, it felt striking that anything I understood about this place seemed to stem from the two-hundred-year-old texts in which I'd once been so immersed. And anything I understood about many things, including reading and writing. Lives get formed in such peculiar ways.

If 'where we swim' is metaphorical, then Charlotte Smith, Frances Burney, and also Mary Wollstonecraft, who felt perpetually unhoused and wrote so often about water, were some of the company I swam with. They were part of the imagined family that inhabited me – and, in this place, especially Smith.

I was shivering now and my skin was rising in goosebumps. I wondered which specific aspects of my understanding of the present these voices from the past had shaped, and what that might have to do with why I – and so many of us – swim.

I'm doing that thing of foregrounding dead writers again. It's not easy to relinquish. And my voice and thoughts sound different in this place. But part of what this book is about is the multiple selves we each contain – uncanny as that feels, at times. Daughter, sister, mother, friend, writer and, here, scholar. I felt a distinctive way in Sussex, and later I decided that embracing the dissonance between selves would be the only way to write this book.

For me, Sussex is Charlotte Smith country. I first came here because I wanted to see the landscapes she wrote about, and we were here again now because of her. Being on this coast and thinking through Smith were one and the same for me.

Smith was a literary celebrity in her own lifetime before virtually disappearing from view for nearly two centuries. When I was in York, walking each day to the 1960s university campus library to study, and then later when I went on to the US, she was an exciting rediscovery. She was fast becoming recognised as the great missing Romantic poet, and changing what the canon looked and felt like. It was thrilling to encounter her life and work in this moment – and a relief to find that here, after all, there were women at the centre of things.

Smith grew up on an estate overlooking the West Sussex Downs and was married at fifteen, or as she put it, sold 'like a Southdown sheep'. From that point onwards, she never had a stable home and moved constantly. I found a way to start writing about her because it seemed that this, too, was a form of movement worth noticing. She published her first poems, a collection of sonnets, in 1783, from the debtors' prison where her husband's debts had the whole family confined. By then she was thirty-four and, staggeringly, had nine living children. I try to remind myself of Smith when I feel constrained by circumstance.

More often than not, Smith's poems worked by conjuring fantasies of solitary wanderings on the South Downs, her 'hills belov'd'. The sonnets she wrote in prison, and which made her name, shifted the focus of the sonnet form itself from the human love affairs of Petrarchan and Shakespearean sonnets to love of the non-human world. Along with Wordsworth's poems of the Lake District, Smith's sonnets helped establish the terms of what came to be seen as classic Romanticism, with its emphasis on nature, childhood and the passing of time.

Again and again, Smith came to her imaginings of nature for solace from the difficulties of adulthood. She had once been a girl walking these hills, and her life since then had changed dramatically, but at least the hills themselves were still there. I'd liked my young adulthood a great deal more than Smith liked hers, but the closeness of the semi-detached brick houses in the streets we'd walked through to get to the beach had reminded me how badly, after I'd moved to an English university dorm room, I'd missed the farm where I grew up.

As it was designed to do, Smith's collection of fifteen sonnets gathered an impressive subscription list, providing her with enough money to get the family released from prison. If nothing else, this says something about the place of poetry in other times. 'Some very melancholy moments have been beguiled' by writing, Smith told her audience in the preface to the collection, hinting at her situation but hiding its seriousness from her respectable middle-class readership. I'd have a few melancholy moments if I were imprisoned in a single room with my nine children. I liked that her reason for writing was clearly double, both financial and for itself. Her story felt all the more important for that. We still, sometimes, hold on to an imagining of the writer as an isolated, inspired genius, their art somehow separate from the conditions in which they actually live. Smith's story illuminated the narrowness of these imaginings.

In 1787 she made the then rare step of separating from her husband and, alongside writing poetry which included more sonnets as well as extended blank verse poems, she wrote nearly a novel a year until her death in 1806. She also took on commissions, noting in one letter that after having had to sell all her books she was having difficulty writing her history of England for young women. (She wrote it anyway.) She had children and then grandchildren living with her for her whole adult life, all of them generally financially dependent on her writing. One of her grown sons came home to her in the first months of the war with France with his leg amputated. When one of her daughters married an émigré from France and died in childbirth, Smith's grief was intensified by her belief that the death was caused by a shortage of money for medical care. During her lifetime, five of her sons also died, one in infancy, one at eleven, one at sixteen, and two of yellow fever in their twenties. Her lack of financial security meant she had to move twenty-eight times in the nineteen years after she left her husband, although when she could help it, she never moved far from this coast. In later years, she was increasingly confined to her sofa by severe, cripplingly painful rheumatoid arthritis. There were no hip replacements, like the one my mother was going to have, available in 1800. And all the while, year after year, in her poetry Smith continued to imagine herself outside walking the Sussex landscape, often looking out from the Downs at this sea.

It can be easy to scorn those who seek solace in nature. What good was escapism going to do? With Smith it would even be possible, if just looking at her poetry in a narrow way, to dismiss her writerly preoccupation with nature as the writer merely answering – and creating – the literary fashion of her times. In stone libraries laddered with ivy I'd been taught a generalised scepticism. I'd learnt to see the problems associated with the inward turn of much nature writing, and its tendency to use the natural world as a means by which to evoke human emotional states. This made nature both separate from us and there *for* us. I'd also learnt to see the historically specific constructedness of Western notions of nature – or what I'd learnt more recently from ecocritical writing to think of as the non-human world. The very idea of 'Nature', Raymond Williams suggested a long time ago, was invented in the Romantic period as the 'thing' that would heal us, it was imagined, from the damage that modern society had done.

Sea-bathing, which became popular in precisely the same moment, was I now thought an almost comically literal enactment of this fantasy of being healed by immersion in the natural world. Dunk.

And here we still were, seeking out the beach. I rolled over onto my front and laid my cheek on the warm rough stones. I should have brought my volume of Smith's poetry down here to rest my head on.

The irony of asking nature to heal *us*, especially now, felt intense. But I knew there was nothing coincidental about the fact that an interest in nature emerged just as industrial capitalism and increasing urbanisation altered the non-human world itself, as well as the ways in which many people lived in relation to it. Eighteenth-century Britain saw an upsurge in literacy. There was the invention of the novel and the public library, the emergence of coffee shops and newspapers. There was plenty to love, at least for those who had access to these things. But in the second half of the century the population of Britain doubled to nearly ten million. Around 1800, London's population reached the one million mark, making it one of the most populous, overcrowded, dirty cities in the world. Who wouldn't need to get out from time to time if they possibly could? Who wouldn't want to take a trip to the seaside?

I thought of what her imaginings of the natural world might offer Smith – or anyone who felt constrained by the everyday. Increasingly, I felt moved by the strength with which thoughts of nature seemed to uplift her. Her writing reminded me why we might need solace – and especially now, as we allow so much of ourselves to be absorbed by work emails and world news and political commentary – and the kinds of places we might go to get it. And that this was not necessarily a turning inward, or a turning away. Nature was something else, something beyond the human or individual self. An impulse towards nature, stillness, swimming, whatever it was, might move outwards to expand and connect.

That's what her later poems did, the ones I'd spent the most time with and was here to think about again.

It felt important to remember, too, that the contemporary environmental movement has its roots in this period. The sense that we need the non-human world is a huge part of our grief amid our own moment of environmental crisis. It is the imagined cure that itself seems headed for an expiry date.

I turned my thoughts again to the hopeful, almost sentient *whoosh, whoosh, whoosh* of those remote windmills. My daughters were shivering as they gathered kelp into a path from sea to towels. None of us wanted to leave.

The kelp was part of a dense forest that once thrived all along this coast. Only small pockets remain. David Attenborough himself had been called in to narrate a BBC segment to support a campaign to save this 'magical underwater forest' from extinction. As a result of fishing, trawling and of practices like dumping sediment close to shore, which blocks the kelp's light, the kelp has dwindled to almost nothing. The creatures associated with it, too – seahorses, cuttlefish, lobsters – have almost disappeared from the coast.

I wondered how the kelp's disappearance changed the water we swam in, and if some of those swimmers two hundred years ago felt it stroking around their legs. Back then, a massage with freshly collected seaweed was sometimes part of the sea therapy regime. On the BBC segment, footage moved from a rare cuttlefish to a dolphin diving and surfacing, to a wavy green, blue and pink underwater garden. A young scientist explained, 'We need these kelp forests. We need them to purify the water. We need them to have the nursery function back. And we need them to reduce localised areas of climate change.' We need them beneath our feet on the beach, to wonder at and squish between our toes. All of us, we need it all.

*

The next day I set out to drive on my own up to the Downs and on to Beachy Head. Smith's final long blank-verse poem, *Beachy Head*, published posthumously in 1807, is considered her masterpiece, and I wanted to see the place again.

I'd been struggling all morning in the small apartment where the group of us was staying. I was having trouble simultaneously negotiating work plans, parenting and partnering, not doing any of them well and resentful of all three. Just occasionally, when I was in this mood, Tim would suggest I go for a run. In the eighteenth century they would have called it a fit of the spleen, perhaps caused by my wandering womb. Women were supposedly subject to such things. As we walked out for breakfast, crossing the footbridge from the spit into the historic town centre, I noted the picturesque boats leaned immobilised in the mudflats left by the retreating tide. Impatience and dissatisfaction pushed at me. I couldn't wait to get away.

As soon as I was driving alone along the esplanade into Brighton, I felt that familiar shift of thoughts slipping gear. It never took long. I had the busy town rising on one side, the opening sea on the other, and I felt immense gratitude for the conditions of my life. There was so often this oscillation between solitude and being subsumed into the busy world of my wider familial unit. It felt possible, in the time and place in which I'd been born, for those of us who are very lucky, to have both – including on the road.

I drove through town, past the elegant Georgian crescent of apartments on the land side and the rebuilt Victorian fairground pier projecting out into the sea. I was thinking about the two women I'd fallen in love with in my year in England – one Brazilian, the other Welsh–Scottish. I still remembered what the woman with whom I thought I might share my whole life, and who moved to America for a while to be with me, wore when she worked the eighteenth-century printing press in our first week together at

York. The two women were now married to each other and lived somewhere here in Brighton.

These were their daily streets, and this was the beach they might wander down to in the evening after work or a dinner out. It was momentarily unsettling. We'd failed to arrange to meet up on this trip, either because we'd mucked up the dates or because it still seemed complicated, even though we'd all got together before. Thinking about B. and M. living together here brought with it a palpable sense of the presence of other possible lives.

But these women were another story. This drive was about my relationship with dead ladies. I was through Brighton and winding my way up into the hills to the east.

A decade before she wrote *Beachy Head*, Smith wrote her poem about exiles from the Revolution. It occurred to me it was set somewhere close to where I was now driving. She'd structured *The Emigrants* around one of her walks and an encounter with a group of just-arrived French families and clergy one bleak morning in the winter of 1792. The exiles sat on the ground looking out at the 'dim cold sea' that now rolled between them and their homes. Nearby, their children gathered shells in a chilly stream while the adults waited to see how Britain would receive them. To return to France at that point would have brought a death sentence. As I entered the pleasant prettiness of the outskirts of Brighton, I thought about how deliberately Smith had rejected the possibility of a nostalgic pastoral fantasy in a timeless landscape. Her poem about the emigrants embodied the fact that the wider world was always already there with you. Nor were things ever simple – Smith had been a vocal public supporter of the early Revolution and these emigrants were mainly Royalists escaping it. But they still needed help and sympathy, she argued in her poem; they were still people who had become unhoused. By the time she wrote this poem, by then in her early forties, she felt that 'nature' as a place merely of retreat from the world was neither possible nor an ethical choice. It wasn't what her continuing to write the natural world was about. The epigraph from Virgil to the second part of the *The Emigrants*, set in 1793, ended: sævit toto Mars impius orbe. 'Throughout the world, Impious War is raging.' War between France and England continued almost without pause for the rest of Smith's life.

Driving east from Brighton, I let the rental car navigation system guide me. It directed me inland but I couldn't zoom out far enough on the digital screen to see the map properly, so I ended up in a new development called Beachy Head View, the place reduced to a GPS location and real estate branding. There wasn't any view as far as I could tell. The neat boxy houses all turned in to face one another. I stopped to ask for help and a man at a corner pub gave me directions. Aware my allotted time alone was dwindling, I drove back towards the actual cliffs at high speed – or at least as high a speed as I could manage on winding English lanes. I wished I'd got the bus instead, but also felt renewed appreciation of having an itinerary set by Smith to push me past where the houses ended.

In *Beachy Head* Smith has her poetic stand-in walking yet again, this time along the distinctive white chalky cliffs jutting out from the South Downs. The poem was written from her sofa in her home, by then small, bookless and far from the sea. But it expands from there into explorations of geology, biology, botany, natural history, human history, time, and individual and collective memory. In it, Smith, a thick-set woman in her mid-fifties who could hardly walk, spoke in multiple voices, from well-read historian to botanist to 'poet' to woman wandering the hills. Her persona was by then popular and recognisable. She'd journeyed a long way from that sold-off Southdown sheep, and also from the young poet recurring to her own lament.

She called *Beachy Head* a 'local poem', alluding to the eighteenth-century tradition of topographical poems dedicated to the description of a place over time. It's not so different from twenty-first-century writing about place by writers like Robert Macfarlane and Kathleen Jamie, and only seemed like a modest claim. In the first of many footnotes that formed a sedimentary layer on top of which her verse rested, she told her readers that in 'crossing the Channel from the coast of France, Beachy-Head is the first land made'. The Battle of Beachy Head in 1690 marked an English naval defeat that played a symbolic role in eighteenth-century histories of invasion. Beachy Head wasn't just any place; it was a border location, resonant with anxiety and vulnerability, but also of connection to other people and places.

I was heading in the right direction finally. The ocean rolled its blue out beyond the green Downs far ahead of me.

In *Beachy Head* Smith started with an image that made the very idea of local or national history feel short-sighted – that of Britain being joined to France and the Continent sometime in the deep past, before being 'torn from it by some convulsion' of the earth. Later in the poem, the speaker finds the fossils of seashells in the cliff, and meditates on a time before these 'chalky mountains' rose out of the sea. To Smith, Beachy Head was the vast 'lapse of Time' made visible. She imagined the wide sweep of human history, as well as her own personal history of loss, becoming insignificant in the face of it.

I drove on through the Downs, with their neat hedgerows and occasional flock of sheep. I thought of Smith walking here as a girl, perhaps before her marriage, and becoming curious about finding shells in the crumbling chalk, some 'quite in a fossil state', others more recent – cockles, mussels, and periwinkles – and some like small land snails. 'It is now many years since I made these observations,' she wrote in another footnote, remembering how the 'appearance of seashells so far from the sea excited my surprise, though I then knew nothing of natural history'. In the intervening years fossils had become a subject of general curiosity, contributing to a shift in how the earth was understood, the specific puzzle of the existence of seashells on cliff tops contributing to the formation of modern geology. Smith had herself written a book on natural history for children and was working on a natural history of birds. Her seemingly idle speculations in Beachy Head are a response to emergent understandings that nature itself had a history. This must have been the kind of adjustment in knowledge, I thought, that entered into one's body in the way understanding of the Anthropocene and climate change is beginning to enter into ours, only perhaps with less dread. By this late moment in her life, Smith was no longer seeking out nature as part of an unchanging world, but imagining it as itself ever-changing. Everything was in flux, just on different scales.

She wanted, too, to evoke the ways in which any place is at once local and global, defined not by its boundaries but by its links to elsewhere. Her speaker looked out at sailing boats and fishing fleets, 'Afar off, / And just emerging from the arch immense', and, less unequivocally positively, at a commercial ship returning, 'richly freighted' from its voyage somewhere in the wider empire, appearing 'like a dubious spot / Just hanging in the horizon'. In a passage that tells of the settling in of evening over the water, the sea-snipe's call 'tells that something living is abroad'. The bird was thought to cross the channel at night, 'flitting near the surface of the waves' and 'uttering a short cry'. There were other lands out there.

What moved me most about such passages was their suggestion of the sheer strangeness of all that is beyond any person's sight and comprehension but to which we are connected. Smith's friend the poet William Cowper evoked the same feeling when he wrote about the uncanny, and still relatively new, experience of reading of far-off events in the newspaper while 'still at home'. In Smith's poem, the images of a travelling ship and a calling seabird, like the fossil shells embedded in the land, made it impossible to imagine a locale that is simply local – and impossible to imagine any nation, place, or human in isolation, either in time or space.

I'd thought a lot about *Beachy Head* in the month in which I kept my own local waterlog on Wellington's south coast. The poem had been with me as I watched planes and whales come and go, rocks pushed up from the water, my own life seemingly lived quietly, even boringly, with my family in a wooden house near the sea on the other side of the globe. I'd remembered it at the Grand Canyon, too. And I'd been surprised by how much I'd been conscious of it as I read the daily Brexit news in present-day Britain.

I turned into the Beachy Head car park and pulled up beside two tour buses.

I already knew something different about this place, from the simple act of coming here again. I had a photo of my by-then ex-girlfriend here on a windswept day on my last visit. But I hadn't remembered how the place opened out not only towards the sea, but into the land, with the Downs themselves sweeping back from the high point of the cliffs, so there was a feeling of space in all directions. So much sea and sky. There was the land, the gentle undulating paddocks, the sheer white dropping away into blue. Both the sublime and the beautiful, to be eighteenth century about it.

But by the time Smith was writing *Beachy Head*, if any present solace was still on offer to her within the natural world it was not to be found in either the inward turn of the solitary wanderer nor in such 'widely spreading views'. It was instead in the labour of paying attention, in the natural history endeavour of 'observing objects more minute'. For her, any hope of consolation or insight was located in the act of 'Wondering' from small parts to 'fathomless' wholes.

I stepped out of the car into the wind. From Smith, I knew the names of birds. She described terns, gulls, tarrocks and grey choughs, for which she provided a list of other names – saddle-back crows, as she says Sussex people call them, but also *Corvus graculus* and Cornish choughs. Choughs, I thought as I stood near the top of the cliff listening to the calls of the seabirds. *Chough, chough, chough.*

Birds flew out and back. What a place to live, to build, and rebuild fragile nests and try to raise young.

If there was any place Smith felt at home in her later life, this was it, on the precipitous edge of these hills where she grew up – on the border between places. I watched a small grey form as it lifted on an air current, as if taking pleasure in its own body and free movement, before it took its chances and dove, disappearing where the white ridge of the cliff met the blue of the sea.

Smith had revisited this landscape in her mind again and again, over decades. As I stood on the 'range of chalky mountains', I was aware of the pleasures accumulated from my own repeated visits to this place, both physically and through rereading.

Before, I'd hardly been able to wade through *Beachy Head* itself. The claims of Smith's mature voice were too thundering for me; her dwellings on the passage of time weren't yet of much interest. There was little in here that my early-twenties self cared to fathom. I'd fixated, instead, on the fact that Beachy Head was a notorious suicide spot, at least since the eighteenth century; hundreds of people have taken their lives here. I paid particular attention to Smith's tendency from her very first sonnets towards fantasies of being 'released by death', an envy of relief from suffering that extended to a macabre envy of skeletons pulled from graves into the sea, and evocations of the ocean being called in over the land to drown her poetic speaker. I was drawn, too, to similarly dark imaginings in Mary Wollstonecraft's writings, especially after she was devastated as Revolutionary France disappointed her hopes for swift social transformation – in particular in the lives of women – and the lover she'd met in Paris abandoned her and their baby. She twice attempted suicide, the second time by jumping at night from Putney Bridge into the River Thames, her heavy skirts weighted with rain.

I now saw that these two writers, Smith especially, had initially been all melancholy wandering to me, their writing resonating with loneliness and with existential as well as literal homelessness. The figure in Smith's sonnets appealed to my younger self almost as much as it did to her devoted contemporary audience. In particular, what made the poems so compelling was the sense she evoked of *missing*. Of something lost, or not quite right. Her signature poems were rightly called *Elegiac Sonnets*. One contemporary rival called her sonnets 'everlasting lamentables', which was a fair comment, although to feel something had been lost wasn't necessarily wrong. But the young me, I think, linked Smith largely, and relatively uncomplicatedly, to the engravings that appeared in one of the early editions of her poems.

The engravings depicted young women, each standing alone, outside in the light of the moon or sitting on a rocky shore with a book, not quite in control of their own lives, and looking very thoughtful about it. I was known to tell people I liked this literature because it wasn't afraid to express feeling – to the point of mushiness. At the time, it didn't seem a very fashionable thing to say, but I felt I had something to learn from it. Despite everything, I still do. Perhaps the stance has even become somewhat more fashionable too. But I can see now that at that stage, it was for me still a highly romanticised image. Apart from anything else, the women in the engravings were *always* young and always lovely. Their melancholy was meant to be observed.

Reading Smith and Wollstonecraft again in preparation for this trip – my whole family coming to this place largely because of this – had felt different. The feeling began to crystallise as I stood there alone on the grass above the cliffs. What I found in these women's writing now was not so much collapse and desolation and loss. It was strength. It was a sense of writing their way towards release into the vast complexity of the world and a single human life lived within it. Smith lay on her sofa writing (furious) letters to lawyers about her children's forever-withheld inheritance (one of the real-life Chancery cases that inspired Dickens' *Bleak House*), and about the pain of her cripplingly swollen joints.

And, at the same time, she was imagining this place, and from it the globe and the history of Earth. I imagined her waking in pain in the night, hardly able to move, and writing herself out onto hillsides.

The wind pushed at me and the sea roared below, and I got as close to the edge as I dared. I saw flights of pleasure opening from the chalky layerings here, with their fossils telling of a porousness between places and times and people, as well as between any moment in one's life and any other. Right then, this seemed like the only possible way to see. My exhilaration – perhaps even mid-life joy – spilled outwards. It was something I was surprised to find I'd brought here with me. It must have formed incrementally over years. I planted my feet and opened my arms to the air like the wings of a windmill, hands and fingers blooming.

Would Smith have bathed in the sea? I didn't know, but it seemed possible. The year Burney recorded swimming in a moonlit dawn in Brighton, Smith was in prison, trying to write her first poems. Jane Austen swam on this coast in 1804, when Smith's arthritis was at its worst. At the time, Smith wrote to a friend of how her breasts were covered in blisters, and she was unsuccessfully trying to raise money to 'go to the sea', sea-bathing having been recommended by her doctor. She added, with a rare flash of humour, that she was 'literally vegetating, for I have very little locomotive powers beyond those that appertain to a cauliflower'. Other times were easier, so perhaps Smith did get into a bathing machine for a medicinal dip.

Regardless, walking by the sea and across the Downs was clearly a kind of immersion for her, as was writing about it. It was akin to sea-bathing. Or, more precisely, the fact that walking and swimming as leisure activities came out of the same historical moment tells us about much more than the commodification of nature. The last time Smith came to this coast was with her granddaughter Luzena, sent by one of her sons for her to take care of. It was the little girl's need for 'sea air' that got Smith to the coast one last time. I hope they came out here to walk together in the wind.

A gull swooped out and down towards the water below and I saw, just beyond, where it disappeared on the horizon, two people in a small boat. I watched the boat pitch in the waves, its red sides seemingly half-submerged then up again and afloat. Wollstonecraft had gone out into the fjords in Norway in a small boat like that one.

I knew Wollstonecraft swam too. I'd edited her beautiful book about travelling through long-stretched Scandinavian summer days with her baby, leaving my own babies with Tim or my mother in our kitchen while I went to my desk and away into other women's lives. Having written her foundational political treatise on women's rights, Wollstonecraft turned to the embodied form of the travel essay, which allowed her to talk about pretty much anything, from social structures and the economics of rocky coastlines to her love for her daughter. The book is written as a series of letters to her unfaithful lover, and she wrote of how, in a small town just south of Oslo, she discovered the 'new pleasure' of sea-bathing. As there was no bathing machine in the town, a young Norwegian woman proposed rowing her across the water to bathe among the rocks. Wollstonecraft first had to learn to row too, because the other woman was pregnant, and she wrote of how her thoughts kept time with the oars as she indulged in 'pleasant forgetfulness'. I imagined the two women learning to move in motion. I imagined them stripping together and lowering their bodies into sparkling water between rocks. Wollstonecraft had left behind her recently weaned baby in Sweden for a few weeks to attend to business here. This wasn't her second daughter, Mary Shelley, whom Wollstonecraft would die giving birth to two years later, but her first daughter, Fanny. Wollstonecraft's Norwegian writings give the sense she was missing her child badly, but just as clearly they evoke a feeling of recovery and expansion. At last she had stretches of space to walk and think. 'Air, exercise, and bathing, have restored me to health, braced my muscles, and covered my ribs,' she wrote. After they swam together, the women let the boat drift. When they plunged their oars into the sea again to return home, they found they were moving through innumerable small purple and white starfish floating just beneath the surface.

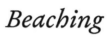

Beaching

Onetangi

as I stretch and bend and bow
their long shafts flare
—Sarah Broom, 'The Skeleton Dances under the Stars'

It is easy to see the beginning of things, but not where their different parts began, or where they will end. The Waiheke ferry was packed. A group of men talking more loudly than anyone else folded themselves into the seats beside us, coffees in hand, ironed, collared shirts, expensive sunglasses on heads, well-cut jaws: Aucklanders bound for a winery tour, letting off that vibe men without their women sometimes do. There were a lot of Gold Cards in the crowd too, off on free day trips courtesy of Winston Peters. We got out our own cards for a family game of Strip Jack Naked. I muttered about the gobbling, monied set, as though we weren't part of it, and Tim pointed out a Waiheke old-timer, sandals and dreads, trying to manoeuvre a piece of boxed-up furniture onto the boat, a woman jostling behind him with an ancient-looking bicycle.

Tim's parents were meant to be with us that day, but as it turned out it was just the four of us. The trip was only forty minutes but on arrival it felt like a remote island, like Great Barrier even, the water surrounded by tree-darkened hills, the crowding line of people eager to land. We transferred from ferry to bus, squeezed swaying with the girls in the aisle. Only then did Tim and I smile at each other across the tops of their heads. We love this place.

Tim, especially, loves this place. His mother bought a bach on the island after her parents died, her mother and builder father having left her a house in an Auckland suburb where owning your own home became a fortune, even three decades ago. The bach became the place where Tim hung out as a young adult, with his parents, and with friends, spending long nights having those new adult conversations, sometimes ending with all-night wanders on the beach. I only knew about this from recounts, of course; it came from his life before me. He was a tramper and caver when we met, and had just published his first novel. He hadn't left New Zealand for ten years and I was living in New Jersey.

We hadn't planned on coming north at all this summer, but on New Year's Eve a function on Google Photos sent me a notification for 'On This Day 2010', and the image materialised unbidden on my phone screen.

In the picture, Tim's mother, Barbara, sits barefoot on a cane sofa at the Waiheke place, one of our daughters under each arm. She's reading what looks to be a Richard Scarry board book about an apple car. Toys are scattered around the floor. Lena and Natasha look very alike. They're at that big-baby, small-human stage, still chubby, but dressed in proper T-shirts and pants, downy hair beginning to form curls on their heads. They look intently at the book, Natasha with her finger in her mouth in concentration. Barbara pivots forward, her face deep in pleasure, as though this is one of the places she always wanted to be.

I emailed it to her and she replied: *That is so beautiful. And we've all got hair.*

Tim and I looked at the photo again, noticing the curls not only on our daughters' heads. After that we phoned to insist we should all get out to Waiheke together, and booked plane tickets. The place wasn't big enough for us all to stay there now that the girls couldn't sleep in a cot pushed up against our bed, but we could bring our tent.

Oral chemo had been 'holding things' for Barbara for a few years, although not her hair. *Holding things* is a phrase doctors say. It spills into the language we use too, as if things really are being held, paused, so we needn't think about them yet.

By the time Tim's father, Mike, picked us up from the airport a few weeks on, Barbara had started a new round of intravenous chemo and this time it had been tough. Mike warned us she was exhausted. She met us in her stylish grey wig as we spilled out of the elevator to their Auckland apartment, the girls rushing in to be hugged by their tall, slim nana. It was a gesture I remembered from visiting my own grandparents.

Before we'd really said hello, the phone began ringing and Barbara set off to answer it. The girls rioted into the room where they sleep in this place – their grandfather's office, filled with books he's written on the origins of language and the human brain, translated into multiple other languages, including in scripts he doesn't recognise. But it wasn't the books the girls were after.

'Micha!' we heard one of them shout in delight.

The three of us looked at each other and laughed.

'They've always loved Micha, haven't they?' Mike said.

Whatever sound the ancient, child-sized bear originally made when you tipped him forward, he now made something like the mewling call of a newborn lamb. Lena and Natasha loved his size, so satisfying to hold.

The three of us drifted after Barbara, who was talking on the phone now, on the threshold between kitchen and living room.

In the natural light, her skin was translucent white, as smooth as porcelain. She was nodding slowly.

We waited in the living area with its views and sense of sky that didn't require one to walk anywhere, and I understood, anew, the apartment had been a long-term move. When they shifted here in their late sixties, they were the young ones in the building. Only Tim seemed to feel the loss of the house in Parnell where he grew up. I had visited a few times but was never part of that chapter of their shared lives. Mike had a seventieth birthday party soon after they moved in, and what seemed distinctly old then now seemed quite young. He was now eighty-two, but still writing books and being flown to conferences; in the car he'd told us about a trip next month to Europe. Barbara, I calculated, must be about to turn seventy-nine.

We heard her say from the kitchen, 'Blood transfusion. Oh.'

And then, 'Hang on. What do you think, Mike?'

I thought of the blood of another person pulsing into one's veins.

Tim's father's back was to us, his hands in his walk-short pockets. He hesitated. 'If they say so, I guess,' he said. But more seemed required. 'You must need it, Barb. They're the experts.'

I glanced at Tim, who was listening, but being careful not to seem to be; I saw how he was cast on the same tall, angular frame as his mother.

He felt unreachable in a way I wasn't sure I'd known before. I felt the intensity of being a part of this family that wasn't my own, and the way in which I was at one remove, as though I could put my arms around him, around them, but there would still be a gap between chest and chest. There was an unspoken grief here, wholly theirs. And yet, the distance between us, and the force with which he became fully visible to me in the moment, made him feel like a part of me. I moved across the room to him.

*

Two days later it was just the four of us on the Waiheke bus. Barbara had spent the day before at the hospital and we knew that our combined exuberant presence in their apartment would exhaust her. We would enjoy the island for them by proxy.

As we swayed on the bus, I was thinking in Venn diagrams. Tim's childhood was in one circle, the culture of my own in another, and our new family of four the set in the middle, made from us.

When Tim and I first met, he drank his tea from a cup his mother had made, a generous rounded shape he held between both hands for warmth in his cold Wellington flat. We had come to the island soon after. My memory of that visit was associated with my father's having invited me to go somewhere with him that week, but this new invitation had felt important, like it could be not just for now but for everything. I'd been in a number of not-so-great relationships by then, including the one with the British woman where I'd got irritable and controlling, and with a man, a fellow graduate student in America who regularly got so drunk he 'forgot' plans we'd made to meet. Hard now to imagine those other lives I might have kept living. I was back home with my parents in Wellington, taking a break from study to try to write. I'd got just old enough to sense when I might have met someone to love.

It was winter on that first visit here; it rained every day, but in hindsight it may have been the first place where it felt possible we could become a couple.

Seventeen years on, the bus still stopped first at Oneroa, still filled with hippie shops selling crystals and tie-dyed clothing, despite the rapid transformation of the island into an Auckland suburb and playground for the rich and retired. Seats opened up and we took them, separate from each other, momentarily two pairs: adult and child. The bus passed the new supermarket in Ostend and down into the dip of mangrove flats.

That first visit here must also have been the first time I met

Tim's parents, although I don't especially remember. Barbara was a potter in the 1970s. We stood doing dishes together in the kitchen of their old house, and I think I asked her about the cup she'd made that Tim now had. Maybe I had an inkling of what it might come to mean to be loved by her son, but I wasn't old enough yet to properly know how to make conversation with a woman from another generation – to see the stretch of a life, and that its chief interest might not come from a profession. Of course, in our generation we'd have it all sorted. Mike and I talked universities. Still do. The cup Barbara made has lost its handle, but it's still on our kitchen windowsill, holding the brightly coloured bits and pieces that end up being treasured in a home with children.

Our stop was the end of the bus run, at Onetangi. We ate eggs and chips in one of the two seafront cafés and then, rather than going up to the bach, stayed on the beach.

It's a whole eco-climate warmer up there, in Auckland itself, and more so on Waiheke. Onetangi is such a tourism-board picture-perfect New Zealand beach it feels almost unreal. The mirage effect was only accentuated that day by the pulsing hot stillness, the long stretch of white sand merging into the blue sea.

We sat on the sand near where a barefoot beach wedding was taking place, with readings in Gaelic and Māori, and talk of two families and peoples coming together. From the amplified speeches, we gathered the couple had met in London. It was a standard story.

'Have you ever thought of living on an island?' the bride had asked.

She meant Aotearoa, we realised, not Waiheke, or the marriage itself. Relationships were a kind of island in themselves – their own separate piece of land.

Tim never asked me that, but there was a sense in which the invitation to be with him was also an invitation to leave another life I was making, and to join him back here.

His parents didn't enquire whether we were going to get married – they don't ask private things like that, or at least they didn't. My own parents did. My mother, I now think, wanted us to have a part of what she and my father have. I'm not sure Tim's parents can have fully trusted me with their son during the four years in which I still lived elsewhere. It must have seemed distinctly possible that I wouldn't, in the end, join my life to his. It certainly seemed so to me at the time.

Now we changed with our children on the sand, piling our clothes beside our overnight backpacks. The four of us walked into the water together, no need for Wellington bravado in this heat. Tim and I just lay on our backs and floated. It was so still. We floated beyond the gentle break, out beyond the girls' depth so they had to swim to stay with us.

It was a long way from the days when the girls would puddle around in the shallows, trying to eat sand and having to be stopped by a grandparent. And further from the time when Tim and I, Barbara and Mike, would sit on the sand here with books, pre-children and so grandchildren. And even further from that first visit, when Tim and I swam together, filled with desire by the warmth of each other's bodies in the freezing water.

When we finally got out and moved further down the beach to the shade of a pōhutukawa, the girls swam in parallel as we walked. Prompted by the wedding we were skirting around, we talked about the stories we'd heard people tell at the weddings we'd been to, all the myths families build up about how relationships come to be. And then how they're sustained – or not – across shifting lives, jobs, houses, children. In theory, we didn't really like weddings. Or at least not the more conventional kind. But still, I was fascinated by them – in what the coming together of different people and families meant. And the leap it took.

In the water, Lena and Natasha befriended a small naked girl whose mother had a surfboard. The three children crawled onto the board while the mother held it still, then a wave lifted them screaming in unison and they rode a frothy white peak right up onto the beach.

Later they found separate spots in the sand to build sandcastles. They kitted the castles out in décor of shells and seaweed, and with moats, which sandcastles must have. The children had been reluctant to come out to the island, saying Waiheke wasn't fun without Nana and Poppop. Once away from them, they were fully absorbed in their own experience.

We were all tired by the time we headed to the house, but we zipped up the steep path. When the girls were smaller it had felt like a lengthy family journey.

The path had been too steep for Barbara for a while now. Apart from everything else, after being on chemo for so long her immunity was too low for the operation she needed on her hip. She couldn't even take the kinds of painkillers that had kept my own mother moving. Unlike Barbara, my mother would be able to have a hip replacement within months.

Last time we were out here, only a year ago, Barbara's vegetable patch was sprouting bundles of zucchini and tomatoes for our arrival dinner. Waiheke was her garden – she spent her weekends out here in the sun, her knees dark with dirt. She also painted the view. This year they'd had the vegetable garden dug out and replaced with topsoil and grass. You could hardly see it had been there.

We scoured the pantry and fridge, finding pasta and leftover cheese and capers. The kids, who were still out on the lawn, could make do with pasta with butter. Tim and I moved around each other quietly in the small yellow kitchen awash with late-afternoon sunshine. It reminded me of the colour of Barbara's hair in the photo.

The night before, in the city, Barbara had said, 'I don't go to the beach anymore. It's not much fun for me. It's too much.'

Two years ago she had said, while watching Lena and Natasha do vigorous running somersaults over the arms of her sofas, 'I guess they won't remember me with hair.'

She's never had any self-pity. Not even in the years when she couldn't sleep for the itching, and had to go for respite care in the hospital, where they wrapped her whole body in something like Gladwrap; not when the radiation burnt off a layer of skin; not when she was sent to Melbourne once a month for an experimental treatment, where they took all the blood from her body and irradiated it with light.

I thought of how I'd never been able to properly say how much I've admired her in these years, her seeming acceptance of life as it is, translated into courage and strength.

The night before, she'd also talked about selling the Waiheke place.

We'd had no idea how to respond. We brushed it aside and moved on.

After the girls were in bed upstairs in their A-frame attic room, Tim and I sat on the deck in the stillness of the evening. It was quiet but for the sound of eighties dance music from the wedding reception, and the sound of sea.

Tim's hands curved tight around a beer. 'I guess we missed it,' he said. The moment for us all being on the beach again together.

The bay was alight with boats, more than we'd ever seen here, each a floating light on the dark water.

The next day, Tim's brother and his wife and daughter – Simone, the third of our girls' three cousins – would come out on the ferry to join us on the island to talk, and a couple of friends who live here would also join us on the beach. Things would get louder. Tim and his brother would stand together on the beach gesturing up at where the bach is obscured by trees on the hill. There will be something similar in the stance of these two sons as they stand with hands on hips above their swimming shorts, wearing sunglasses and peaked hats, thirty or more years on from when they shared a home. They are two men dealing with things, and the agreement they're coming to is that there is no need to decide anything yet.

To imagine selling the house would be to admit to an end. To admit that we are living in narrative, not a loop. But talking about a house is easier than talking about a mother's illness – about the pain in her hip, the colour of her skin, or seeing that, for the first time, she sat while we cooked for her.

And there's something else too, which is the awkwardness that comes from imagining the bach as money. Beside us on the beach Tim's old friend and the friend's partner and small daughter will be getting out of their togs and back into clothes to leave. These friends live here on the island and each time we visit they talk about how they might not be able to stay, because of rising rents. Inherited inequality is already the reason we own our own home in Wellington, whatever our proclaimed politics; both our families contributed money. It will feel wrong in so many ways.

They will all decide to hold on to the house for now.

For weeks, I will think of Barbara – the pain, the itching skin, the blood transfusion, the aching, aching hip. I will think about how long she's been living like this, and of how she might be right – her grandchildren will not remember her with hair. When I saw the photograph, I realised that I didn't quite, either. Although perhaps in time the photograph will replace the memory.

But soon some of the sadness settles, and what I will feel most acutely is the shift in lives. It is like the aftermath of sound, as though for a moment I could actually hear the sea. Or like a retreat back up a tributary stream, moving away once more from the ocean's roar. The intensity of the memory is heartache. It is Tim standing with his brother looking up and then away; it's an earlier memory of Barbara and our daughters with their feet in the frothing sea; and it is Barbara without her wig, ghostlike in a white nightie in the early hours. We had woken her, still adult children needing keys to borrow her car. It is the exhaustion on her face later that day, as though she couldn't do this forever. But mostly, it is Tim, and the cleaving to him I feel, and the understanding that he, too, will get old, and I with him.

If we could talk about the things she would like to do again, would Barbara want to swim? Mike goes in every day when they do make it out to the island. In the summer months he swims slow lengths at Parnell Baths in town, as he has had to give up running. His own artificial hips are decades old.

At one point, when we are all talking again about the bach and about how she doesn't swim anymore, and she really 'just sits up at the house', Barbara will say, 'Perhaps I should make myself.'

Perhaps we could go together at night, I think, with no one to see.

But it's hard for me to imagine making such a gesture, in reality. Maybe it's not mine to make. Or perhaps it's that I am like her, my all-but-mother-in-law: too careful sometimes of leaving space for other people's emotions, rather than stepping forward in response.

My mother and a friend she loved who was dying went together and simply lay on the grass, looking up at the sky.

The next summer when we come up to Auckland, Barbara will still be very much with us. The doctors will have decided to cease the chemo, meaning she can now have an operation to fix her hip. They will have got to Waiheke again a few times, although we won't manage to coincide. Instead, we will head out with the kids and instructions to water the kōwhai she's planted where the vege garden was. And I still haven't asked. Although I have shown her this. Of everything I have written in this book, it is what I most wonder about having written, and whether it is right.

My not asking is also because it is not only her I imagine swimming now, but also Tim and me, entering the depths, naked, skin thin over our skeleton bones, as though what has become visible is our own mortality and all the life stretching in between. I imagine us, another lifetime on, holding each other, on the island. We are swimming together in one long, staggering dance of transfused blood and bone, our children far away behind us on the beach.

Ordinary Animals

In Wellington, the last week of the summer school holidays was hot – really hot. Tuesday broke records. Australia was also hot. Australia was having the hottest summer on record again, with back-to-back heatwaves and temperatures in the high 40s. There were uncontrollable fires, mass fish deaths, health warnings about going outside, and fruit cooking on trees. Much of North America was in the grip of a polar vortex, bringing life-threatening windchill. A friend emailed me from a plane grounded by snowstorms.

But things were fine here in Wellington, where summer being a bit warmer is a good thing. There was something uncanny about it. When we exchanged pleasantries with friends – 'Great summer!' – it was often with a provisional laugh, as though we thought this couldn't last but didn't really believe it wouldn't.

The world is burning. And yet, here we were in it.

On the most blistering day, Tim texted me at work in the mid-afternoon and an hour later I was on my bike. It was even hotter out of the office, where I'd spent the day with emails and online video meetings. There was a soupy thickness to the air.

I took the still vigorously opposed cycleway down the valley to the South Coast. It was pure pleasure to career down the road, warm air pulsing past, hills rising on either side, right through to the sea road and along to Princess Bay, where we most often swim. Our local. On the way, going through the shops, I zipped up onto the pavement to escape the exhaust of a stopped bus, hot and rasping in my face. Then, when I dropped back into the stream of traffic, a driver started honking at me.

I was jolted into a moral fury. In my work dress, still hurtling along the road, I gave a finger to the back of the car as it shot by, much too close.

'Fuck off,' I shouted, trying to steady the wobble of my bike. 'Bastards.'

I shook my head. I remembered how, once, a woman had opened a car door at traffic lights and clipped me on the neck, toppling me, my ribs crashing into the side mirror of a parked car, the pain in my chest. Every cyclist has a story like that one.

'Fucking bastards,' I shouted.

I pedalled on.

I thought of our new electric car, just back from the panel-beater after being crashed into by an enormous black Toyota Hilux ute. They 'just didn't see us', they said. I wanted to kick every large black vehicle that passed. There were a lot of them. New Zealand has the highest rate of car ownership in the OECD, and the fifth-highest greenhouse gas emissions per capita, although nearly half of that's from agriculture. So much for what we believed about our environmental purity.

But even I found my personal piety annoying. Besides, there were all those flights we'd taken over the past two years. And my own fear of cyclists when I'm behind a wheel on a narrow road.

It was a familiar stream of thought, hemmed in on either side, like the hills funnelling me now towards the sea. My anger began to drain away, along with the exhilarating jolt of us versus them. And I felt only the vulnerability of a human frame on a bicycle, whirring in flight along the verge of the narrow road, but also again, slowly, persistently returning, that pumping pleasure in the day.

It was cooler the moment I hit the sea road. Even without a breeze, water cooled the air. I cruised around the bay beside the still ocean.

After I'd locked my bike behind the changing sheds, I spotted Tim and the kids among crowds of children and adults – the parents released from work and glad of this gasp of sea air. The holiday extended.

I kept my sandals on and picked my way across the burning sand to my family.

'It's like a European beach today,' Tim said, offering me a towel to wrap around myself while I changed.

It was. It felt like the Mediterranean – warm and still, with groups of people standing in the sea talking.

We were more used to watching a few kids running in and out of the cold water screaming. This isn't an ice-cream beach. There's no dairy or café, nothing here but rock and sea, and wind more often than sun. Near us a group of teenagers lounged, one girl propped up on her elbow in a tiny yellow bikini, the boys lying back, all of them pretending not to be aware of this revelation of each other's bodies.

We had a spot beside the piece of driftwood at the centre of the bay, a bare log that had washed up from somewhere. Lena and Natasha waved to us. They were in the midst of a group of school friends, all leaping about on the rocks. Then they pulled their goggles on and plunged into the water, swimming out to what they'd been calling Jacuzzi Island, a rock with a warm dish of a pool. Not that they really knew what a jacuzzi was. We watched them pile into the pool like small animals wallowing in the heat.

Earlier in the week they'd taken fish identification charts with them and swum between the rocks, coming back with stories of spotties and tiny yellow-grey triple fins.

There had been rumours all month of a pod of dolphins off the coast. From time to time we searched the still water beyond. I lay back and felt the heat prickling the length of my skin. This is happiness, I thought. And also, this is home.

We got in the water twice and stayed until evening. Finally, we loaded my bike on the back of the car and drove over the steep hill towards our house. We kept having to slow right down to edge past carloads of people on their way to the water. It was like a video game – people hurtling at each other in an effort to get at the sea. Windows down, tanned arms, sunglasses and flowery shirts. As Annette Lees writes in *Swim*, it's like sleeping or eating. In Aotearoa, swimming is *what people do*. On that day it felt as though the sea was all that any human could ever want or need.

We didn't get to the beach for the rest of the week. On Saturday, we had a friend of the girls' around who had an injury and temporarily couldn't swim. I got grumpy, as I do when I can't get out. The kids couldn't decide what to do. I went to the garden to dig up the last of the agapanthus, down to the roots, and when I came back in, my hands sticky with clinging residue, the kids were still niggling at each other. I ended up muttering stuff in the general direction of Tim, who was outside reading. I don't mind digging the agapanthus, but I can't do everything. Farcical. I'm not much good at fighting, and as I said it I knew it wasn't fair or true. The very deckchair Tim was sitting on, with its striped yellow-and-white canvas made from a recycled tablecloth, he'd sewed with the girls as a holiday project. They were all very proud. The love always took over. But still.

He eventually came inside to help Natasha get going on some sewing project, and we were up and running again, until the sewing machine jammed.

I texted the parents, some of my best friends, asking where they were. It was a short-tempered message.

We pulled up YouTube videos on bobbin threading, and I pushed my way into the sewing seat while Tim held up his phone and the girls continued scrapping in the background.

'I'll do it,' I said. 'Clockwise. Like that. Hold the phone closer.'

It still didn't work. The listless, hot children left us, and the mess they'd made, and headed out to climb the pūriri tree.

In the quiet, I looked up across our living space. It was set up with the leftover detritus of a Harry Potter dormitory and a cascade of Lego among half-built and then abandoned buildings, and now the floor around our feet was awash with scraps of dyed material. We were aflood, our world channelled into this small dysfunctional machine. I was gripped by a sense of panic, ready to shout at just about anyone.

Only after five did we manage to get to the beach. Tim stayed to keep trying to fix the sewing machine, and to cook dinner. I imagined he needed a break from me. I did.

As the girls and I tipped the hill before the descent, we could feel the wind shaking up the car. Our house was sheltered and we hadn't registered the southerly whipping in off the sea. Today Princess Bay looked like what it was – a thin line of sand and rock between steep hillsides and the ocean. A place deserving of a different name.

The car park was almost empty. There was no one in the water, just a few buffeted people on the beach. One group had a wind shelter. The water looked choppy and uninviting.

But I was glad. The rugged beach had returned. I'd been reading David Wallace-Wells's *The Uninhabitable Earth: A Story of the Future* and kept thinking about his observation water is not a 'beachside attraction for land animals'; it's 70 per cent of Earth's surface, Earth's predominant environment. The ocean was the subject, the main character here; it was us who were transitory figures dipping in. We'd been returned to our true size.

The water was cold. I needed a few countdowns from the girls this time, and I missed the first two in my reluctance to leap. But then I dived through the skein of a low wave and stayed under long enough for the water to take and float my body, and there was that familiar wash of life, of pleasure, the tingle of skin, the rush of blood to organs, as my body literally pumped itself alive.

I left the girls in the shallows and went further out, doing my clumsy version of breaststroke through the breakers. I kept going until I was really in among the waves, with no view of the hills. The beach itself washed in and out of sight, just blue-green water. I let myself drop under, forcing my eyes open against the salt, the churned-up water. I was alone.

The sea could have me, I thought. There was a definite tug, a pull towards the ocean, and away.

When I came up for breath, the girls were calling and gesturing.

'Too far, Mum,' Natasha shouted.

As a wave passed, I saw her there standing in her new spotty cheetah swimsuit, planted firmly in the water, beckoning me in.

'Mama.'

Her voice was insistent, almost strict; I felt its throatiness across the waves.

As I began to push in, there was a hint of fear at the pull of the wave going out. I made it in some way on the incoming waves, then they pulled at me as they sucked back. But gently. It was just the insinuation of a tug from the depths. And all that water between us.

But then I was back and could stand again.

Lena and Natasha joined me as I headed into shore. They were like fish, like eels, like seals, diving and slipping through the water, brushing their slick bodies against me. I would have liked to have been able to carry them on my back, as whales do.

'It's wonderful,' Natasha said, her teeth chattering. Shivering is good; it helps your body keep itself warm.

The next day was Sunday. The last day of the school holidays. We walked through the town belt, along the spines of the hills, past the girls' school, to the coast. We went up through the eucalypts with their naked grey trunks – past blackberry bushes, where the girls stretched their arms to get the last plump berries missed by dog-walkers, and I tried to remember lines from a blackberry-eating poem I teach by Galway Kinnell about 'the silent, startled, icy, black language / of blackberry-eating' at the end of summer.

At the peak, we could see the Kaikōura Ranges again to the southwest across the strait, and the bare, sculpted hills to the west. At the new water reservoir, we stood among plantings of flaxes and grasses in reds and browns and greens.

'Mum,' Natasha said, taking my hand. 'How high will the sea be in fifty years?'

I felt her exact height beside me. She was the right height for me to stand and hold her hand, as though to say – you're nine, don't worry, the adults have got this one. There's an order to these things.

Except, of course, I didn't say that. I looked at where she was looking, down over the Rongotai isthmus, with its houses, schools and airport, all built on land raised not so long ago by geological upheaval, decisively pushed up from the sea only in the earthquake of 1855. This is the place where the taniwha Whātaitai tried to force his way out of the harbour to find his brother who had swum away.

Tim and I glanced at each other.

'I don't know, love,' I said. 'Higher.'

After the 2016 Kaikōura earthquake, whenever I walked the girls to school I would look out and imagine how a tsunami would roll in across the isthmus, right through to the harbour.

The week of the quake, a friend from Canada moved into a brick house down on the flat and spent the night with her baby and husband in their car in the hills. Three years later, they were looking to sell their house and move to higher ground.

But I know it's a different kind of fear, this imagining of a sudden rush of water. I'd been reading climate change fiction lately, and I hate it when books do this – going for the sudden excitement of the apocalypse, the water flooding in like in *The Day After* – rather than evoking the slow, complicated process it seems more likely to be. Or imagining what we could do to stop it, or survive it. 'Apocalypse comes swiftly and charismatically … climate change occurs discreetly and incrementally, and as such, it presents the literary imagination with a series of difficulties: how to dramatise aggregating detail, how to plot slow change.' I'd read Robert Macfarlane quoted on this in several online pieces recently. The essay of his, written back in 2005, was called 'The Burning Question'. On New Year's Eve of 2019, as we watched news of fire sweeping across Australia, it seemed it might, in fact, be swifter than we'd thought.

But perhaps thinking about earthquakes and tidal waves really was like thinking about climate change. After the earthquake, it was easier to imagine an altered Earth, the shifting of the ground on which we stood. Now we knew how the hills could shudder, how the beds in which we woke could sway like small boats. I'd stood in the doorway in the dark with the one daughter I'd managed to pull from her bed, shouting at the other to stay where she was in her rocking bunk. Later, the thing she would remember was that I got her sister, but not her.

'Mum?' Natasha was pulling at my hand.

We were moving on, Natasha darting off to catch up with the others. But now I was occupied by thoughts of how my daughters imagine.

The scale is impossible to understand, even as an adult. The stretch of a human life has been put in a new relation to the changes of Earth, which we'd imagined previously as incomprehensibly slow.

I'd been reading writers' meditations on deep time too, including Macfarlane writing about the vastness of Earth time as compared to the human instant; the Grand Canyon or the cliffs at Beachy Head were like Earth's cross-cut diagram, evocations of the geological sublime. Macfarlane also writes of the 'ethical lotus-eating' comfort this intimation can seem to offer, when instead it should be a 'radical perspective, provoking us to action not apathy', making Earth eerily alive. He writes of a 'web of gift, inheritance and legacy'. I think of kaitiakitanga, of which I still have so small an understanding.

But then as Wallace-Wells writes, 'The perspective changes when history accelerates.' Instead, there is something like 'a feeling of history happening all at once': 'You can find it already by watching footage of an iceberg collapsing into the sea.' Or, by your children not asking about the past, but about the future of their adulthood. Timothy Morton calls climate change a 'hyper-object', a conceptual fact too large and complex to comprehend. Wallace-Wells writes, 'The facts are hysterical.' The facts are exponential. In 2020, we would all begin truly to learn what 'exponential' meant.

It was scorching hot on the hilltops we were walking now, the harbour below to the north, to the south the whole blue-green ocean.

I'd read in my newsfeed that morning about the Waiwhetū Aquifer, the reserve beneath the harbour which supplies 40 per cent of Wellington's water supply. I'm not sure I'd known it existed or thought about where our drinking water comes from. That cross-cut diagram, which I only half understood, deposited layers of greywacke, gravel, marine beds, sea, and fresh water beneath my shallow imaginings of the harbour.

I caught up with the others and tried to tell Tim about the undersea vents I had read about, but everyone was singing on, literally.

The aquifer releases pressure via the vents through the hard clay of the harbour bottom. Beneath, the gravels of the aquifer itself were laid down by the Hutt River, Te Awa Kairangi, nearly half a million years ago. But the vents. If the aquifer is drawn upon too heavily, as it regularly comes close to being in dry summers, or if sea levels rise, then the vents will become in danger of releasing seawater *into* the aquifer. In 2018, the equivalent of 9300 Olympic swimming pools were sucked out; demand is predicted to rise by 60 per cent by the end of the century. By then, if we continue on our business-as-usual approach, global sea levels are predicted to rise by as much as a metre. Some studies suggest much, much more. It was unclear what the plan was. My throat was dry.

We were still on the exposed path and my actual children, rather than imagined future ones, were pulling at my attention.

Lena was pink in the heat. 'But you promised it would be shady.'

Always, the promise. Kids remembered.

Tim laughed. 'It will be. Look, just down there.'

Her shoulders drooped; she was an early expert at parental blame for how things turned out. In time there would be plenty of ammunition for it.

But Tim was laughing at her; he's better than I am at making both girls laugh their way out of things. And at making me laugh too, pulling me out of my tendency towards cataclysmic thinking. Knowledge occupies him differently.

There is certainly something numbing about the incessant predictions of doom. Something off-putting, too, about the excitement that I sensed some commentators felt in terrifying us all with visions of 'cascading violence, waterfalls and avalanches of devastation, the planet pummelled again and again' – a projected spectacle in which everything is a drama of different forces doing battle, the sea a killer. It doesn't help much with the question of what to do, even while something draws me into Wallace-Wells's imaginings of his child, in the future, living through 'the greatest story ever told'.

'You're having such a good chance to complain,' Tim said to Lena now and she almost laughed.

Her shirt was gloriously stained with blackberry juice. I could have licked her then – and Tim too.

I'd had conversations recently with younger colleagues at work about whether they should have children. 'Fuck climate change,' I'd said at the end of one, unable to imagine we were really there. But there was the genuine ache of it, raised and felt when coming from a woman in her mid-thirties.

I thought about all these conversations over the coming months, in particular when I went with Lena and Natasha and my parents on the first of the children's strikes for climate action. We walked beside girls in blue school uniforms with neat ponytails and masks covering their mouths. Written across the masks were the words *Exit Generation*. Another girl walked stumblingly in a box up to her waist painted the colours of the ocean, emblazoned in black lettering: *This is what two feet sea rise looks like*. Behind us two gangly boys sounded out chants in deep voices, new instruments even they seemed surprised to hear resonating from their chests. *What do we want? Climate justice*. But it was the *two, four, six, eight, save the world, it's not too late* sung by my daughters and thousands of other children and teenagers that really got me.

I wanted to say to them, you're the best thing that's happened for a long time. I stood beside my own mother and father in the crowd outside parliament and cried when a sixteen-year-old girl gave a speech. I was remembering being at similar marches when I was the age my children are now, and I was wondering what I'd done in between – and what we hadn't. My parents' environmentalism had seemed admirable, but optional. On a visit to them soon after the march, my father showed me a poem he wrote in the 1980s about Earth's warming.

What were the effects of inhabiting this sense of doom? In myself I notice a dissonance in long-term thinking, so that discussions of ten-year concerns at work, or even five-year plans, can feel like make-believe games. How did those teenagers feel when released from the embrace of a march, when they were alone in the vast spaces of their beds at night, trying to imagine careers and sex and families and a world of unknowable futures?

The possibilities for climate grief, environmental depression, eco-anxiety, felt all too real, too pressing, too present. Perhaps it was closer to climate paralysis.

Instead, I wanted to add volume to those newly resonant voices.

It was on the bus home from that first march that news of the Christchurch mosque shootings began to pulse in on the phones everyone was suddenly holding in their hands. It was a spray of hatred, puncturing the lungful of hope the march had gathered.

I'm still unsure whether I shielded my own children too much, or not enough, from the full understanding of what happened, and from all the grief and conversation that followed about what it could mean. How, that afternoon on 15 March 2019, a white supremacist man walked into places of worship in Christchurch and shot and killed fifty-one Muslim men, women and children, and injured forty-nine.

Among so many other things, it was a violent reminder that we were not all in this together. People carried different losses and different hates. At times over the past two years I've felt that Princess Bay and the hinterland valley behind it in which we live are too safe, too homely, too sequestered. The mosque shootings shook that certainty, at least for a time, altering my sense of how quickly things can change. I wasn't sure anyone would ever again be able to pretend that here in Aotearoa New Zealand people are safe, as if we're removed and insulated in some special way from the world. A myriad of underheard voices came forward to try in grief and rage to explain that, given this country's history of colonialism and racism, this shouldn't have been new knowledge. The shooting was a shock only to some of us.

It became impossible to look at these hillside gullies, seas and sweeping skies, and not see the need for an adjustment in vision. As though the scenery didn't fit together anymore. For a fraction of time, the majority seemed to be listening to those who were trying to explain. The majority where, in this sense at least, I lived. For that moment, we were all shaken.

Some people, of course, had been shot and killed. Others lost mothers, fathers, sons, daughters.

Our children will carry this. I hope they can understand it better than we try to. I thought again of those teenagers from every school in the city, home from their hopeful march, videos streaming out at them from their phones.

We were starting to walk down off the hilltops. The sense of dread receded again into the background.

We entered a temporary shade as we dropped down further, a coolness smelling of earth and fallen leaves. Lena and Natasha ran way ahead, singing a song about a school of killifish: *Who are the teachers here, and which ones are the kids?*

We followed them down through the ngaio and scrappy mānuka, the path crisscrossing an empty streambed then spilling us out on the tinder-dry grass by the playground.

Finally, we reached the crashing water. It was rising in enormous waves this time, great steady blue walls of it. We crossed the road at the giant bronze propeller. It was from a decommissioned naval vessel, sunk in 2005 somewhere out there for divers to explore, a small premonition of a sunken world. The propeller's gorgeous, petal-shaped fin-blades, even in their hefty stillness, gave the impression of motion. There were plenty of real shipwrecks further around the coast towards Red Rocks, Pariwhero, too, the origin of the distinctive red of the rocks at once geological and mythic. They are red because they were formed from basalt lava when the Australian and Pacific plates collided 250 million years ago. And they are red because the ancestral explorer, Kupe, cut his hand when he was gathering pāua, or because his daughter threw herself from the clifftop when he failed to return from a journey of exploration. And they are red with the blood Māui used to bait his hook when he fished Te Ika-a-Māui, the North Island, up out of the sea.

I tried not to think about the fact that the ocean now has dead zones the size of Europe, the sea itself suffocating as well as rising to pull the land back in.

At Houghton Bay, which the girls' school is working hard to restore to its Māori name of Haewai, there are signs warning against swimming. *Strong undertow.* There was a great, rolling surf, the waves huge, regular and steady, breaking white and alive with surfers. The waves curled in and we could see a figure inside one, her white tail plume disappearing and reappearing as she came out on top. Two teenage boys, their bodies slick and dark in wetsuits, tumbled onto the beach then plunged back into the sea.

The four of us leapt across small chasms of churned-up water between rocks to reach Princess Bay. It was almost a party scene over there, as many people as there had been on Tuesday, but today the beach was shrunken as the tide had pulled up. The waves were huge in a way we weren't used to. Usually the precise curve of rock protected us but now the storm was close, though not yet close enough to feel, still happening under a blue sky.

We found a group of friends and set up towels behind the

driftwood. Lena and Natasha went straight for the water, but even they paused at its edge. When Tim and I joined them, the girls let themselves be knocked over in the shallows. They seemed, in moments like this, to have no fear. Each wave drained back with a roaring rattle of stones being turned, pulled, rearranged. I stood until a wave pulled me in too, tumbling me down, my breath caught in my chest.

Back on the beach, when an especially big wave came in we grappled for our stuff and there was a collective gasp and cheer. As the tide rose further, the usual polite gaps between towel towns were further compressed. We sat close together with former strangers on the shrinking beach, our heads bare to the sky.

I'd been reading about the monuments, cities and whole cultures that, like sunken ships, will likely be transformed into underwater relics by the end of this century. Lower Manhattan, Venice, Kiribati, Tokelau. Much of the infrastructure of the internet could be gone in decades. In a century: *any beach we've ever visited.*

Every time I heard someone in Europe or North America announcing they will no longer fly so as to avoid the carbon emissions, I thought of the distance between here and there. Between me and my brothers, between my parents and their sons and grandchildren. It would mean the end of family as we know it. Another thing I was far from ready for. Not yet. But what *will* make me (us) ready?

How to imagine the scale of a single human life against the scale of water? How to balance the value of each? How to inhabit the simultaneity of haunting dread and everyday joy? From this space of persistent oscillation, might we come to intimate the urgency for collective action, and collective care?

Another body of water tossed at us, and we all laughed in wonder at the sea, even as it rolled in. The beach was a crowded grandstand. It was audience-participation theatre, in which we would all be called upon. The kids joined us for handfuls of chips and watermelon, salt and juice. They pushed in close, and there was something stunning about the way we were all out there together, watching the waters rise.

Waterlog

Wednesday 26 February, 2020

I head out after the girls are in bed. I dress warmly and drive up over the hill and down towards the coast, while the sky still holds its colour, deepening every minute as it takes on the black. The slivered moon whitens within dark blue.

At last, a night swim.

A few camper vans are parked near the rocks, pairs murmuring at their open back doors, mugs in their hands. A man and a woman sit on a car's bonnet, watching stars appear. Three hundred and fifty years ago John Milton described the night sky, looking up in the moment he stood on the planet, as the 'vast Sublunar Vault'. Everyone down here is facing south towards Antarctica, the hills and houses at their backs. Across the hook of the bay, a double-decker bus moves along the barely visible coast road like a lit-up ship, floating its passengers through the night. The size of whales is often given relative to that of buses, as though fifty or sixty of us could fit inside one.

The calm quiet in the now chilly air – and the intense beauty of the night – is only accentuated by the presence of other people. I hadn't expected company when imagining the wine-dark sea from inside my house. The surprise of close-to-home places could keep on unfurling forever.

Then a 'turd taxi' rumbles by on the road behind, and I feel the sludge of knowledge of the burst sewage pipes in the central city over Christmas. The trucks are working twenty-four hours a day to transport shit to the dump instead of the sea until the pipes can be fixed. The water at this beach has been declared clear – I've checked – but the truck brings a literal stench. That in turn brings with it the memory of watching the orange haze sky from here during the height of the Australian wildfires over the new year.

But the sand is cool under my feet and in the dark the water's gleaming surface is easier to see as surface, with whole worlds beneath.

I've finally got a pair of goggles. Earlier in the day I went diving with the girls. We held our breath, kicked our legs, and floated down, seeing small striped fish flickering their way through groves of seaweed. How could I have got so far and swum so much and only just begun to really put my head under?

In the dark, I watch how the almost-breath of waves comes and goes, not quite straight, instead pushing sideways. The almost imperceptible movements of a chest.

I hadn't quite wanted to leave the ease of home tonight – not really. I take off my jacket, then top and jeans. I'm reluctant to actually get into the water. Why do this – why take off layers, casing, seal? Why make oneself? Why even consider exposing limbs and hair and goosebumped skin to the sea? Why hold out my breathing life – and that of my family – like this, when one could just have stayed at home?

But it has turned out I need this – this stripping down, this immersing. It feels necessary to keep attempting it. It doesn't now feel possible to live a life of only footpaths beneath one's feet.

I leave my clothes on the beach.

The water hardly moves around my legs. I stand for a long time thigh-deep. The temperature of my legs comes to match the temperature of the water. I *feel* warm. I stand still so long a hand-sized fish leaps out of the water near me, twisting a small silhouette of life. It's possible to believe fish jump in joy.

When I dive under, water tumbles along my neck and back, taking everything. I push out, and within moments when I drop my legs the ground is gone, there is only salty water, unfathomably deep. Above, the sky and moon. I push out into the future of my life, of my children, and of this watery planet.

Coda

Monday 20 April, 2020
The book was mostly written. It was about a life that was passing, and about unknowable futures. But everything vibrates differently now.

Three weeks after my night swim, both my brothers had to cancel long-planned trips to visit us all here. I have no idea when we will see each other, especially Tom, who couldn't get here from Colombia even if he wanted to, and where the situation gets harder each day. We visited my parents the day before things really shut down here, travelled together in the same car to walk in the bush, the girls swimming naked in a small stream. We hugged them goodbye, and only then let the anxiety nudge its way in about whether we could have infected them.

Four days after that, we were in lockdown. No driving, except to the supermarket where we stood in lines two metres apart. No physical interaction with those beyond our household. The girls home with us. We talked about bubbles, the small units of one to five people moving a wary distance from other bubbles that passed, edging off the footpath onto roads where there were now only a few cars. With borders closed, New Zealand has become a whole new kind of island, in some ways separated off after all. No touching. Auckland unreachable. I may as well be as far from my parents as my brothers are, their home a short but illegal drive away around the harbour's curled mouth.

A few days into the lockdown we went on a bike ride along the south coast, and when we took a break Tim and the girls stripped and briefly went into the water in a secluded gap between rocks. We returned home to a headline news story featuring an image of a woman steaming through the water, drops of spray pealing behind her curved arm. Below her was the headline: *No Swimming*.

Only fish and whales swim out there now. Birds swoop without planes in the skies, pumping out their own hot paths of breath.

On my phone I look at exponential graphs of viral spread, and networks of connection. If her, then her and him, and possibly you. If me, then maybe that older man's mother. The grid lines spread out in tangled tendrils of life and death. We see it. Properly. As infection. Or not.

We have this moment, inexplicably terrible and new, to take everything in before we push ourselves out again into the connective chaotic splendour and danger of this world. We have a breath to reconsider where and with whom and why we swim, and the ways what we do ripple out into the lives of others.

If it's a chance to learn again, it's one where we will still carry so many things, including our young on our backs. We know how to float, how to spit out water when it floods our lungs. That there are stages in a human life, and in the life of a planet. And that there are choices in what we do.

Tuesday 28 April

We are at the beach before nine the day swimming begins again. The sun is bright, the sky a perfect pale autumn blue. The waves run in across the stretch of a low tide. There are what Natasha and Lena call ankle waves. We keep careful physical distance from a man carrying a kayak up from the beach. When we wave he beams at us: 'It's beautiful out there.' We start the long walk into the water.

Over the coming days there are hundreds of us. We walk quietly, distant but connected, feeling the water washing around us, rising from feet to knee to thigh, all of us wanting, wanting to find ways to live.

Notes

p. 1: 'Gone Swimming': I first wrote about the swimming journey alluded to in this piece in an essay of the same title (*Landfall* 234, Spring 2017, 22–31). I chose to pass through Mōkau in part because of Geoff Park's writing about the locale. I was reading Catherine Knight's history of New Zealand rivers as I drove, and this informed my sense of the present and ongoing impacts of farming, and the ways in which the effects of agriculture on waterways today is different from that of nineteenth-century bush clearances. As Knight notes, cattle have gone from 2 million in 1975, to 4 million in the mid-1990s, to 6.7 million in 2014 as a result of the dairying boom. Huge expansions in irrigation, subsidised by consecutive governments, have drained rivers and streams and in turn intensified land use around them, leading to increasing waste. Even seemingly clear water running off farmland after rain is filled with damaging nutrients, bacteria and other chemicals. The pollutants have just become harder to see. Knight argues rivers need to remain – or be returned to – whatever status we collectively decide is appropriate for their roles, whether that be for generating electricity, for carrying away waste, for 'scenic value', or for hosting various forms of life, such as kanakana. As Knight frames it in her account, our collective lack of management puts many of our rivers in danger of becoming incapable of being 'working' rivers of any kind. I have also been influenced by Tina Ngata, Paul Tapsell and others writing on Wai Māori, and the way these discussions are explicitly framed in the language of 'care', emphasising the need to return the mauri – energy balance – to whenua and rivers and people. For additional understanding of words in te reo Māori used within the text, see maoridictionary.co.nz.

p. 121: In his 2005 article '"Solastalgia": A New Concept in Health and Identity', Glenn Albrecht describes solastalgia literally as 'the pain or sickness caused by the loss or lack of solace and the sense of isolation connected to the present state of one's home and territory'. It is the existential grief caused by environmental change or loss.

p. 165: The epigraph is from Sarah Broom's poem 'The Skeleton Dances under the Stars', *Gleam* (Auckland University Press, 2013), 16.

p. 165: 'It is easy to see the beginning of things, but not where their different parts began, or where they will end': This line is an echo of Joan Didion's: 'It is easy to see the beginnings of things, and harder to see the ends' from her essay 'Goodbye to All That' (first published 1967), *Live and Learn* (Harper Perennial, 2005), 176.

p. 190: There are many stories associated with the distinctive red of the rocks at Pariwhero. The ones to which I allude appear in Chris Maclean, 'Wellington region – Early Māori history', *Te Ara – The Encyclopedia of New Zealand*, 1 August 2015 (teara.govt.nz/en/wellington-region/page-5) and in the information panels at Te Kopahau Reserve Visitor Centre, at the entrance to the walk to Pariwhero.

I would like to generally acknowledge all the writing that has taken me on swimming journeys besides my own; it has been a pleasure to strike out into this genre. This reading has contributed to my understanding and knowledge of swimming – where it comes from, how it feels, and why we care. In particular: *Waterlog: A Swimmer's Journey through Britain* by Roger Deakin (Vintage, 1999); *Swell: A Waterbiography* by Jenny Landreth (Bloomsbury, 2017); *Turning: A Swimming Memoir* by Jessica J. Lee (Virago, 2017); *Swim: A Year of Swimming Outdoors in New Zealand* by Annette Lees (Potton and Burton, 2018); and *Swimming with Seals* by Victoria Whitworth (Head of Zeus, 2017).

For other inspiration, I am especially indebted to the following works and resources: some are referenced or quoted from directly, others provided me with valuable factual information or shaped my thinking.

Gone Swimming

'Can I Swim Here?' Land, Air, Water, Aotearoa (LAWA), lawa.org.nz/ (accessed Feb.–May 2017).

Knight, Catherine. *New Zealand Rivers: An Environmental History.* Canterbury University Press, 2016.

Ngata, Tina. 'Wai Māori: A Māori Perspective on the Freshwater Debate'. In *Mountains to Sea: Solving New Zealand's Freshwater Crisis*, edited by Mike Joy, 18–29. Bridget Williams Books, 2018.

Park, Geoff. *Ngā Uruora: The Groves of Life – Ecology and History in a New Zealand Landscape.* Victoria University Press, 1995.

Tapsell, Paul and Alison Dewes. 'One World, One Health, One Humanity – Whenua, Rongoā, Tangata'. In *Mountains to Sea: Solving New Zealand's Freshwater Crisis*, edited by Mike Joy, 65–90. Bridget Williams Books, 2018.

'Water Quality Swimming Maps'. Ministry for the Environment, mfe.govt.nz/fresh-water/freshwater-management-reforms/water-quality-swimming-maps (accessed March 2017).

Days Bay and *The Whale*

Adam, Pip. *The New Animals.* Victoria University Press, 2017.

'Deep Vein Thrombosis (DVT)'. Mayo Clinic, mayoclinic.org/diseases-conditions/deep-vein-thrombosis/symptoms-causes/syc-20352557 (accessed Feb. 2019).

Gawande, Atul. *Being Mortal: Medicine and What Matters in the End.* Profile Books, 2015.

Grace, Wiremu. 'Ngake and Whātaitai the taniwha of Wellington harbour'. Te Tāhuhu o te Mātauranga, Ministry of Education, eng.mataurangamaori.tki.org.nz/Support-materials/Te-Reo-Maori/Maori-Myths-Legends-and-Contemporary-Stories/Ngake-and-Whataitai-the-taniwha-of-Wellington-harbour (accessed 15 July 2019).

Jenner, Lynn. 'Thinking About Waves'. *Griffith Review 43: Pacific Highways*, edited by Julianne Schultz and Lloyd Jones (2013): 105–12.

Lessing, Doris. 'My Father'. In *A Small Personal Voice: Essays, Reviews, Interviews*, edited by Paul Schlueter, 89–101. Flamingo, 1994.

Mechen, Johanna, Angela Kilford and Aliyah Winter. *Wairua, wairua*, 25 Feb. 2017 to 4 March 2017, Commonground Festival 2017: Groundwater. See angelakilford.com/wairua-wairua

Stewart, Matt. 'Days Bay water chute thrills: 150 years of news'. *Stuff*, 23 Sept. 2015, stuff.co.nz/dominion-post/capital-life/72349735/

Summers, Julie. *Stranger in the House: Women's Stories of Men Returning from the Second World War*. Simon and Schuster, 2008.

Medellín and *Amazon*

Alsema, Adriaan. 'Is Medellin on the brink of another war?' *Colombia Reports*, 27 April 2018, colombiareports.com/is-medellin-at-the-brink-of-another-war

Harindranath, Arjun. 'City on Clampdown: Who's behind the increased violence in Medellín?' *Bogota Post*, 25 April 2018, thebogotapost. com/city-on-clampdown-whos-behind-the-increased-violence-in-medellin/29389/

Lapidus, Sarah. 'Deforestation in Colombia: The forest is burning'. *The Bogota Post*, 6 Nov. 2018, thebogotapost.com/deforestation-in-colombia-the-forest-is-burning/33098/

Mazzanti, Giancarlo. 'España Library'. *The Arch Daily*, archdaily. com/2565/espana-library-giancarlo-mazzanti/ (accessed 5 March 2019).

Reardon, Sara. 'FARC and the forest: Peace is destroying Colombia's jungle – and opening it to science'. *Nature*, 12 June 2018, nature.com/articles/d41586-018-05397-2

Romero, Simon. 'Where Is the Amazon Rainforest Vanishing? Not Just in Brazil'. *The New York Times*, 30 Aug. 2019, nytimes.com/2019/08/30/world/americas/amazon-rainforest.html

Soares, Marília Facó. 'Ticuna'. *Povos Indígenas no Brasil, Instituto Socioambiental*, June 2008, pib.socioambiental.org/en/Povo:Ticuna

Warnock-Smith, Alex, 'Story of cities #42: Medellín escapes grip of drug lord to embrace radical urbanism'. *Guardian*, 13 May 2016, theguardian.

com/cities/2016/may/13/story-cities-pablo-escobar-inclusive-urbanism-medellin-colombia

Arizona

Amundsen, Fiona and Tim Corballis. *Human Hand*, video and still photo installation with text, Dowse Art Museum, Lower Hutt. 2020. See dowse.org.nz/exhibitions/detail/human-hand

Arcosanti. Cosanti Foundation, 2017, arcosanti.org (accessed 2018–2019)

Bishop, Elizabeth. 'The Moose'. In *Complete Poems*, 173. Chatto and Windus, 1997.

'International Ice Swimming Association Swimming Rules and Regulations'. International Ice Swimming Association, internationaliceswimming.com/iisa-rules/ (accessed 16 Feb. 2020).

Keith, Kelsey. 'Architect Paolo Soleri's daughter Daniela recounts childhood abuse in open letter'. *Curbed*, 15 Dec. 2017, archive.curbed.com/2017/12/15/16781940/paolo-soleri-abuse-daughter-arcosanti

McWhortor, Patrick. 'Updated Statement on #MeToo and Foundation Policy'. *Arcosanti*, Dec. 2018, arcosanti.org/metoo/

Robbins, Jim. 'In Era of Drought, Phoenix Prepares for a Future Without Colorado River Water'. In *Yale Environment 360*, 7 Feb. 2019, e360.yale.edu/features/how-phoenix-is-preparing-for-a-future-without-colorado-river-water

Ross, Andrew. *Bird on Fire: Lessons from the World's Least Sustainable City*. Oxford University Press, 2011.

Soleri, Daniela. 'Sexual abuse: It's you, him, and his work'. *Medium*, 14 Nov. 2017, medium.com/@soleri/sexual-abuse-its-you-him-and-his-work-88ecb8e99648

Visit Phoenix. visitphoenix.com (accessed 15 June 2019).

Vagnozzi, Alexa and Grace Fenlason. 'Arcosanti: An Urban Laboratory', avagnozzi.atavist.com/futureofarcosanti (accessed 1 Sept. 2019).

Wainwright, Oliver. 'Story of cities #35: Arcosanti – the unfinished answer to suburban sprawl'. *Guardian*, 4 May 2016, theguardian.com/cities/2016/may/04/story-cities-35-arcosanti-paolo-soleri-desert

Walker, Nicole. *Sustainability: A Love Story*. Mad Creek Books, Ohio State University Press, 2018.

Walters, Joanna. 'Plight of Phoenix: How long can the world's "least sustainable" city survive?' *Guardian*, 20 March 2018, theguardian.com/cities/2018/mar/20/phoenix-least-sustainable-city-survive-water

Perth

'About Naturescape'. Botanic Gardens and Parks Authority, Government of Western Australia, bgpa.wa.gov.au/kings-park/area/naturescape/about-naturescape (accessed 14 Oct. 2019).

Albrecht, Glenn. '"Solastalgia": A New Concept in Health and Identity'. *PAN: Philosophy, Activism, Nature* 3 (2005): 41–55.

Bradley, James. 'Writing on the Precipice'. *Sydney Review of Books*, 21 Feb. 2017, sydneyreviewofbooks.com/essay/writing-on-the-precipice-climate-change/

Bradley, James. Keynote Address. Climates of Change, Australasian Association of Writing Programs, 1 Dec. 2017, Flinders University, Adelaide.

Carmody, James and Jacob Kagi. 'Extinction Rebellion protesters take to Perth CBD, blocking St George's Terrace'. *ABC News*, 11–12 Oct. 2019, abc.net.au/news/2019-10-11/extinction-rebellion-protesters-take-to-perth-cbd/11594964

Cunningham, Sophie. 'Age of Loneliness'. In *City of Trees: Essays on Life, Death and the Need for a Forest*, 269–291. Text, 2019.

Giggs, Rebecca. 'Whale Fall'. *Granta* 133: What Have We Done (Autumn 2015), edited by Sigrid Rausing: 45–53.

Monbiot, George. 'Let's abandon climate targets, and do something completely different'. *Guardian*, 29 Jan. 2020, theguardian.com/commentisfree/2020/jan/29/climate-targets-committee-on-climate-change-report

—. 'Stop eating fish. It's the only way to save the life in our seas'. *Guardian*, 9 May 2019, theguardian.com/commentisfree/2019/may/09/seas-stop-eating-fish-fishing-industry-government

Morrison, Scott. 'Scott Morrison brings a chunk of coal into parliament'. *Guardian*, 9 Feb. 2017, theguardian.com/global/video/2017/feb/09/scott-morrison-brings-a-chunk-of-coal-into-parliament-video

'Net migration eases back towards 2015 level'. Statistics New Zealand, 21 September 2018, stats.govt.nz/news/net-migration-eases-back-towards-2015-level

Riley, Harriet. 'Endlings'. In *Best Australian Essays 2017*, edited by Anna Goldsworthy, 19–24. Black Inc., 2017.

Rottnest Island. Rottnest Island Authority, Government of Western Australia, rottnestisland.com/ (accessed 18 Oct. 2019).

Scott, Kim. *Benang: From the Heart*. Fremantle Arts Centre Press, 1999.

Taylor, Matthew and Jonathan Watts. 'The Polluters. Revealed: the 20 firms behind a third of all carbon emissions'. *Guardian*, 9 Oct. 2019, theguardian.com/environment/2019/oct/09/revealed-20-firms-third-carbon-emissions

Upton, John. 'Ancient Sea Rise Tale Told Accurately for 10,000 Years'. *Scientific American*, 26 Jan. 2015, scientificamerican.com/article/ancient-sea-rise-tale-told-accurately-for-10-000-years/

Weintraub, Karen. 'These Whales are Serenaders of the Seas. It's Quite a Racket'. *New York Times*, 7 Jan. 2019, nytimes.com/2019/01/07/science/whales-songs-acoustics.html

'Western Australian Mineral and Petroleum Statistics Digest 2018–19'. Government of Western Australia, Department of Mines, Industry Regulation and Safety, 2019, dmp.wa.gov.au/Documents/About-Us-Careers/Stats_Digest_2018-19.pdf (accessed 25 Nov. 2019).

Wilson, M. Thomas. *Stepping Off: Rewilding and Belonging in the South-West*. Fremantle Press, 2017.

Zerbini, Alexandre N. et al. 'Assessing the recovery of an Antarctic predator from historical exploitation'. *Royal Society Open Science* 6, no.10 (16 Oct. 2019), doi.org/10.1098/rsos.190368

Sussex

Burney, Frances. '20 November 1782'. In *The Early Journals and Letters of Fanny Burney* vol. 5: 1782–1783, edited by Lars E. Troide and Stewart J. Cook, 175–76. McGill-Queen's University Press, 2012.

'David Attenborough: Save Sussex's magical kelp forests', *BBC News*, 29 Sept. 2019, bbc.com/news/av/uk-england-sussex-49853729/david-attenborough-save-sussex-s-magical-kelp-forests

Dolan, Elizabeth A. 'Charlotte Smith Story Map', Romantic Circles, 15 June 2018, romantic-circles.org/reference/charlotte-smith/map

Goodman, Kevis. 'Conjectures on Beachy Head: Charlotte Smith's Geological Poetics and the Ground of the Present'. *ELH* 81, no.3 (2014): 983–1006.

Horrocks, Ingrid. *Women Wanderers and the Writing of Mobility, 1784–1814*. Cambridge University Press, 2017.

Morton, Timothy. *Ecology without Nature: Rethinking Environmental Aesthetics*. Harvard University Press, 2007.

Owen, Charlotte. 'Round-head Rampion', Sussex Wildlife Trust, 16 June 2017, sussexwildlifetrust.org.uk/news/pride-of-sussex

Smith, Charlotte. *Charlotte Smith: Major Poetic Works*, edited by Claire Knowles and Ingrid Horrocks. Broadview Press, 2017.

—. *The Collected Letters of Charlotte Smith*, edited by Judith Phillips Stanton. Indiana University Press, 2003.

Sutherland, Eileen. '"A Little Sea-Bathing Would Set Me up Forever": The History and Development of the English Seaside Resorts'. *Persuasions*, no. 19 (1997): 60–76.

Williams, Raymond. *The Country and the City*. Chatto & Windus, 1973.

Wollstonecraft, Mary. *Letters Written During a Short Residence in Sweden, Norway, and Denmark*, edited by Ingrid Horrocks. Broadview Press, 2013.

Onetangi and *Princess Bay*

Goodell, Jeff. *The Water Will Come: Rising Seas, Sinking Cities, and Remaking the Civilized World*. Little, Brown, 2017.

IPPC 2019. *Special Report on the Ocean and Cryosphere in a Changing Climate*. Intergovernmental Panel on Climate Change, 2019, ipcc.ch/

srocc/ (accessed Dec. 2019).

Kinnell, Galway. 'Blackberry Eating'. In *Perrine's Sound and Sense: An Introduction to Poetry*, 10th edition, edited by Thomas R. Arp and Greg Johnson, 227–28, Harcourt College Publishers, 2001.

Knight, Catherine. *Beyond Manapouri: 50 Years of Environmental Politics in New Zealand*. Canterbury University Press, 2018.

Macdonald, Nikki. 'Underground water reservoirs at risk from seawater contamination'. *Stuff*, 2 Feb. 2019, stuff.co.nz/environment/109503698/ underground-water-reservoirs-at-risk-from-seawater-contamination

Macfarlane, Robert. 'The Burning Question'. *Guardian*, 24 Sept. 2005, theguardian.com/books/2005/sep/24/featuresreviews.guardianreview29

—. *Underland*. Penguin, 2019.

Milton, John. *Paradise Lost* (1674). Book 4. In *The Riverside Milton*, edited by Roy Flannagan. Houghton, 1998.

Morton, Timothy. *Hyperobjects: Philosophy and Ecology after the End of the World*. University of Minnesota Press, 2013.

OECD Environmental Performance Reviews: New Zealand 2017 Highlights. OECD, 2017. oecd.org/environment/country-reviews/ Highlights_OECD_EPR_NewZealand.pdf (accessed 15 June 2019)

OECD, 'Environment at a Glance: Climate Change'. Environment at a Glance: Indicators, 17 Dec. 2019, oecd.org/environment/environment-at-a-glance/

Priestley, Rebecca. 'Prepare to be Kind (or Melting Ice, Rising Seas)'. *Granta* 153: Second Nature (Autumn 2020), guest edited by Isabella Tree: 192–210.

Wallace-Wells, David. *The Uninhabitable Earth: A Story of the Future*. Penguin, 2019.

Acknowledgements

Thanks: To my families, for letting me write stories that include you, and for responding with such generosity to my attempts to express something about how the world feels to me. To my parents, as always, who hold us close and let us go. To my brothers, poles either side of me. To my new families: parents-in-law, sisters- and brother-in-law, nieces and nephew and beyond, for entering our lives. In particular, I want to acknowledge the generosity and kindness of Barbara, who passed away in late 2020. We miss you. And thank you Tim, Lena and Natasha – I couldn't be happier to have you as my pod. Thank you for your enthusiasm for taking the waters with me, and for oceans of love.

Thanks: To all the people who have talked with me on buses, in canoes, on walks and in the water. In particular, I am grateful to Angela Kilford in Te Whanganui-a-Tara, Laura and John in Medellín, Walter and Claudio in Amazonas, D. in Arcosanti and Nicole Walker in Arizona. In some cases, I have not used full names for reasons of privacy and have also chosen not to name some locations.

Thanks: To the cafés on the southern coast of Wellington where I wrote most of this book, and sometimes stayed too long.

Thanks: To Massey University, for a work home and a grant to help finish what must have seemed an odd book. To my students and colleagues – in particular, Thom Conroy, Tom Doig, Gigi Fenster, Laura Jean McKay, Jack Ross, Elspeth Tilley and Bryan Walpert – from whom I have learnt so much about writing. To audiences in Princeton, York, and the Island Bay Surf club, with whom I talked about the project, in particular Claudia Johnson, for asking what about the sublime, and

Sophie Gee and Esther Schor for perfectly timed encouragement.

Thanks: To my extraordinary writing group, for nurturing the book around our favourite kitchen table: Kate Duignan, Elizabeth Knox, Sarah Laing, Kirsten McDougall, Emma Martin, Sue Orr, Susan Pearce, Emily Perkins and Anna Smaill. To Elizabeth Gray, Nikki Hessell, Sarah Ross and Claire Knowles, for all the years of talking about women wanderers with me. And to the NonfictionNOW family, who helped me see the wider waters into which I was writing.

Thanks in particular to those who read the full manuscript from start to finish and helped me curate its shape and sentences: Kate Duignan, Tina Makereti, John and Virginia Horrocks, and especially Tim Corballis, who lived it in a number of ways.

Thanks: To Victoria University Press: Fergus Barrowman, Kirsten McDougall and in particular Ashleigh Young, for her extraordinary editing. This book wouldn't exist at all without a number of pivotal conversations early on. Thanks also to my agent, Martin Shaw, as well as Madonna Duffy, Cathy Vallance, Sally Wilson, and the team at University of Queensland Press, for also embracing the book and giving it another life.

And finally, thanks to the water, the elks and whales, who turned away, encouraging me to follow. In gratitude.